Power Learners Handbook For College Success

2nd Edition

The Mindset and Methods to Master Your Courses and Earn Your Degree

Peter D. Lenn, Ph.D.

www.PowerLearners.com

Table of Contents

Welcome

The purpose of this handbook is to help you succeed in college. The book presents some specific methods for learning various subjects quickly and easily. The book contains exercises for you to practice those methods, so you will be able to use them in your other courses from now on. Using those methods will get you better results.

But more important than specific techniques, this book will guide you in experiencing these key truths about yourself and your learning.

- I am intelligent enough to master my courses.
- Professors, teachers, books and videos guide me on what to learn and how to learn it.
- I must do the learning, primarily by practicing.
- When I get stuck, getting help promptly saves time and frustration.
- Mastering today's lesson makes tomorrow's faster and easier.
- Getting smarter is motivating and fun.

Perhaps, like many of the students who have been in our courses, your experience with school has been difficult and discouraging. You may worry that you lack the intelligence, interest, motivation or concentration for college. But almost all students of this course learned both that they can succeed and how to do it. You can, too.

You may have volunteered to take this course. Or it may be a requirement you would not have chosen. Either way, I have a suggestion. Decide to master every lesson. If you do, you will gain the methods and mindset to succeed in college.

Lesson 1

The Mindset of

A Power Learner

This lesson is about how you learn and get smarter. You will experience being a Power Learner and how satisfying that can be.

Objectives

In the next 30 minutes or so, you will learn:

- How this course operates.
- The keys to working smarter, not harder.
- Mastery Learning works for you and feels great.

How This Course Operates

In most college courses, you receive information in class and by reading textbooks. Then you memorize, analyze, rehearse and practice in your room or the library. This course is different. In this course, you are going to practice and study in class. Your professor will not lecture or lead discussions. Instead, like a coach, he or she will guide and help you as you practice and master best-known-methods for learning other courses.

In this course or any other, it is both useful and legitimate for you to get help while studying, so long as you persevere in practicing until you can demonstrate mastery on your own. Whenever you need help, you can ask the professor or a classmate. Then, you continue practicing until you have mastered each technique and lesson. If a classmate asks you for help, you can help or say no.

Practice

Where do you do most of your learning in a regular course?

- In class
- At home
- In the library

Where do you most of your learning in this course?

- In class
- At home
- In the library

Feedback

Where do you do most of your learning in a regular course?

- In class
- **<u>At home</u>**
- **<u>In the library</u>**

Where do you most of your learning in this course?

- **<u>In class</u>**
- At home
- In the library

How You Learn?

Learning is a change in your brain that enables you to do something you could not do before. You cause those changes by practicing what you are learning to do. The right practice strengthens certain synapses in your brain, creating pathways that allow you to remember, think and act in new ways.

Many people, including students and faculty, think of college courses like an IQ contest. The professor instructs; the smartest kids remember the most and do better on the tests. Homework may seem like a sideshow. But homework is where students do the problem-solving, writing, memorizing and analyzing that produce most of their learning. In fact, about 80% of your learning occurs when you do your homework. So, Power Learners focus on homework. The main things you will learn in this course are:

- You can master your courses by doing enough of the right kinds of practice.
- As you do, you will become smarter, learning faster, with more motivation and confidence.

Practice

Which of these activities results in most of your learning?

- Listening.
- Watching.
- Reading.
- Practicing.

About what percentage of your learning happens when you do that activity?

Feedback

Which of these activities results in most of your learning?

- Listening.
- Watching.
- Reading.
- **Practicing.**

About what percentage of your learning happens when you do that activity?

80%

Instruction, Practice and Feedback

The main ingredients in schooling are instruction, practice and tests. Instruction is when you receive information from professors, books and videos. Instruction prepares you to practice. Practice is when you actively recite, write, analyze or solve. Feedback is information you get from others and maybe from yourself on how you are doing. To be sure you are clear about these three things, here is a practice exercise.

Practice

For each of the activities listed in the table below, put an X in the column to indicate whether the activity is an example of instruction, practice or feedback.

	Instruction (Get Info)	Practice	Feedback
Listen to a lecture			
Take notes in a lecture			
Watch a video			
Do a chemistry experiment			
Read textbook			
Engage in a class discussion			
Listen to a class discussion			
Solve problems			
Write an essay			
Outline a chapter			
Drill with flashcards			
Check answers in the back of the book			

Feedback

Here are our answers. If you differ on some of these, that's fine, so long as you understand how we use these terms in this book.

	Instruction (Get Info)	Practice	Feedback
Listen to a lecture	X		
Take notes in a lecture	X		
Watch a video	X		
Do a chemistry experiment		X	
Read textbook	X		
Engage in a class discussion		X	
Listen to a class discussion	X		
Solve problems		X	
Write an essay		X	
Outline a chapter		X	
Drill with flashcards		X	
Check answers in the back of the book			X

Mastery

Most subjects move from simple facts, ideas and skills to more difficult ones. If you master the early lessons, you can handle what comes later. If you don't, the course becomes more difficult.

As an example, consider learning arithmetic. You start with addition, then subtraction, multiplication, and so on. If you have mastered addition, it will take less time and effort to learn subtraction. If you try to learn subtraction before you've mastered addition, learning subtraction will take longer and be more difficult. In the same way, once you fall behind in a course, it is very difficult to catch up.

This graph shows that mastering each step decreases the time needed for learning the next. In other words, as your knowledge of the subject builds, your learning rate zooms upward.

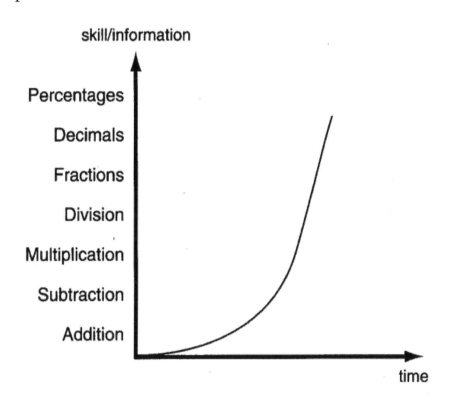

Our learning curves have the same general shape but are not identical. Learning curves vary for many reasons, including the subject, age, experience, attitudes, and how you feel on a given day.

Mastering a skill means that you are competent to perform or demonstrate that skill. Having mastered addition means you are ready, willing, and able to pass any reasonable test in adding. You could show others how to add.

With Mastery Learning you also retain the material longer. And mastering the material gives you a sense of progress and success. So, college becomes much more pleasant and satisfying. You may start to enjoy learning subjects that previously were difficult for you.

Mastering an assignment always takes longer than just getting it done. Still, that extra time is a good investment because it will save you even more time on later assignments. So, over a full course, mastery learning takes less time.

As you will discover later in this lesson, the extra time to master an assignment can be surprisingly little. Often it will take just another 5 or 10 minutes.

In most classes, professors can't stay on a topic until everyone has mastered it. So, in conventional courses, you must manage your study outside of class to master each assignment.

Practice

1.) To master a skill means that:

- You are one of the best in the world at that skill.
- You did your assignments.
- You can demonstrate the skill when asked.
- With a little practice and a little luck, you could pass a test on that skill.

2.) An accurate definition of managing yourself for mastery is:

- Practice every day.
- Do your assignments on time.
- Know what the goals are and practice until you reach them.

3.) If you master every lesson as you go through a course, you can expect your learning rate for that course to (increase/decrease/stay the same) _____ (select one to fill in the blank).

Therefore, with Mastery Learning you may need (more/less/the same) _____study time for the whole course (select one to fill in the blank).

4.) Is everyone's learning curve for a particular subject the same?   Yes or No?

5.) Differences in learning curves between people arise from differences in:

- Intelligence.
- Related experience.
- Previous practice.
- All of the above.

6.) Based on what you've read so far, do you think you have enough intelligence to master all your courses?   Yes or No?

Feedback

1.) To master a skill means that:

- You are one of the best in the world at that skill.
- You did your assignments.
- **You can demonstrate the skill when asked.**
- With a little practice and a little luck, you could pass a test on that skill.

2.) An accurate definition of managing yourself for mastery is

- Practice every day.
- Do your assignments on time.
- **Know what the goals are and practice until you reach them.**

3. If you master every lesson as you go through a course, you can expect your learning rate for that course to (**increase**/decrease/stay the same).

Therefore, with Mastery Learning you may need (more/**less**/the same) study time for the whole course.

4.) Is everyone's learning curve for a particular subject the same? **No.**

5.) Differences in learning curves between people arise from differences in:

- Intelligence.
- Related experience.
- Previous practice.
- **All of the above.**

6.). Based on what you've read so far, do you think you have enough intelligence to master all your courses? **We hope you said, "Yes."** If not, the rest of this course may change your mind.

What Do You Want to Improve?

When looking at ourselves, we have some choices. One is to focus on what **should** be:

> I should be better at reading.
> I should have studied more last semester.
> I should be better at taking tests.
> I should have been born at a different time.
> I should weigh less.

The list can get so long it is discouraging. A second option is to forget "what I should be" and turn to "where am I today." That means telling the truth about what's happening right now—no shame, no blame. Telling the truth frees up energy and sets the stage for personal change.

The Personal Profile below is a way to size up how things are for you right now. It is not a test. Rather, it is a way to ask yourself important questions and tell yourself the truth about the kind of student you are today. Use the Personal Profile as an opportunity for noticing the things you do well, along with the areas in which you want to improve.

PERSONAL PROFILE

Rate each of the statements as

> 5 = always or almost always true for you.
> 4 = often true
> 3 = sometimes true (about half the time)
> 2 = seldom true
> 1 = never or almost never true

GOALS AND PLANS

I know my long-term goals.
I know my short-term goals.
I have written down my goals.
I base my actions on my goals.
I plan my time and activities.
I write down my plan.
I keep track of appointments.
I am on time.
I have adequate time for my various activities.
I keep track of my grades in school.

STUDY SKILLS

I take useful notes in class.
I can study from my notes.
I participate in class.
I know what to study for tests.
I take tests well.
I master the material in my courses.
I review my homework, tests, and papers.
I study effectively from textbooks.
I know how to study for each course.
I can write effectively.

HOMEWORK

I write down my assignments.
I have the supplies I need.
I have a regular place to study.
I have a regular time to study.
I can concentrate.
I don't procrastinate.
I keep my papers organized.

MOTIVATION AND ATTITUDE

I am motivated in school.
I like learning.
I feel smart and able to succeed in school.
I like my teachers.
I like school.
I feel good about my achievements and learning in school.
I feel confident.
I can rely on myself to do what I say I will.

HEALTH AND WELL-BEING

I am healthy.
I get enough sleep.
I eat well.
I am happy.
I get along well with friends.
I get along well with my family.
I get along well with teachers.
I tell the truth to others and myself.
I feel good about myself.
I have confidence in my own abilities.

If you wish, put a star or check next to just one, two or, at most, three things to focus on improving.

The Power Learner Mindset

Here are some comments on the main ideas of the Power Learner Mindset.

1. I am intelligent enough to master my courses.

Your IQ is defined to be fixed by your genetics, regardless of how much you have learned. Research shows that almost everyone's intelligence is adequate for college success. Whether you succeed depends primarily on doing enough of the right practice. As you learn, you get smarter. If you learn a new language, you are smarter than before. The whole idea of education is to get smarter by learning.

2. Professors, teachers, books and videos guide me on what to learn and how to learn it.

How do you think about teaching? Do you think you are supposed to understand, remember, and apply knowledge just by listening and reading? Consider, instead, that teaching prepares you to learn.

3. I must do the learning, primarily by practicing.

Everybody does. No one ever became good at anything without practicing. The work of learning includes answering, reciting, analyzing, writing and solving.

4. When I get stuck, getting help promptly saves time and frustration.

If possible, call a professor or a classmate immediately, then continue practicing.

5. Mastering today's lesson makes tomorrow's faster and easier.

Learning is cumulative. Knowing how to add helps you learn how to subtract. Mastering Spanish 1 paves the way for mastering Spanish 2. Mastering today's assignment sets the stage for tomorrow's assignment. The extra time invested today pays back even larger time savings before the semester ends. Be sure you know everything you need to know at the beginning of each class. If you don't, drop the class. It is rarely possible to catch up during a course.

6. Getting smarter is motivating and fun.

Practice

Memorize these statements of the Power Learner Mindset following the directions below.

- I am intelligent enough to master my courses.
- Professors, teachers, books and videos guide me on what to learn and how to learn it.
- I must do the learning, primarily by practicing.
- When I get stuck, getting help promptly saves time and frustration.
- Mastering today's lesson makes tomorrow's faster and easier.
- Getting smarter is motivating and fun.

Directions for Memorizing

- Read the statements once to get the general ideas.

- Start with the first statement. Read it; then look up and try to say it from memory. (If you're in the library or a class, speak under your breath.) If you get stuck, look at the page for a prompt. Then look up and say it.

- Continue practicing until you can recite the first statement from memory—word for word, without looking at the page, and without stumbling. Mastery is reciting the statement as quickly and easily as you can say the alphabet: A, B, C, D, etc. Master the first statement before working on the second one.

- Memorize the second statement. When you have the second statement memorized, work on reciting the first and second statements together.

- Once you have the first and second statements mastered, start on the third one. When you have mastered 1, 2, and 3, add the others, one at a time, until you can rapidly recite all six word-for-word.

Mastery Criteria

As you complete each lesson in this program, get together with your professor to check that you have mastered the new skills. If both you and your professor are satisfied that you have reached mastery, then you're ready to move on. If not, together you can figure out what other actions might bring you to mastery.

For this first lesson, mastery is for you to recite the six statements of the Power Learner Mindset, from memory, word-for-word, rapidly. You are also to be able to explain the Power Learner Mindset in your own words.

Lesson 2

Managing Your Time And Your Life

How are you at managing your time? Are you spending your time on the things you need to and want to? Are you wasting time procrastinating? This lesson will help you plan, get things done, and still have time for work, sleep and fun.

How Are You Spending Your Time?

A good first step toward better time management is to look at how you are spending your time now. Of the 168 hours in a typical week, how much time do you spend sleeping, in class, working and socializing? To help you with that, there is a TimePlan form available online.

Practice Follow these directions to open the form.

TimePlan Spreadsheet

You will use the TimePlan spreadsheet for this exercise. Here are directions for two ways to download the TimePlan spreadsheet from the Internet.

Recommended Method: Use a Google Account

- If you have Gmail, you already have a Google Account. If not, sign up for a free Google Account at https://accounts.google.com/SignUp?hl=en
- Sign in to Google Drive at www.Drive.Google.com using your Gmail address and password.
- In a new browser window, go to this URL:

    https://goo.gl/3LNSAb

The TimePlan will open as a View only file.

- Click on the File menu at the upper left and select Add to My Drive. You will now have your own editable copy of TimePlan in Drive.

Alternative Method: Download to your own computer

- In a browser window, enter this URL: https://goo.gl/3LNSAb
  The TimePlan will open as a View only file.
- Download the file to a folder on your computer as an xlsx file.
- To open, edit and save your TimePlan.xlsx, use a spreadsheet program such as Microsoft EXCEL or the Google Drive app.

Feedback You should have this TimePlan spreadsheet on your computer.

Weekly	Schedule						
	Monday	Tuesday	Wednesday	Thursday	Friday	Saturday	Sunday
6 a.m.	Sleep	Sleep	Sleep	School	Sleep	Sleep	Sleep
6:30 a.m.	Sleep	Sleep	Sleep	Sleep	Sleep	Sleep	Sleep
7 a.m.	Wash & Dr	Wash & Dr	Wash & Dr	Wash & Dr	Wash & Dr	Sleep	Sleep
	Eat	Eat	Eat	Eat	Eat	Sleep	Sleep
8 a.m.	Commute,	Commute,	Commute,	Commute,	Commute,	Wash & Dr	Wash & Dr
	School	School	School	School	School	Commute,	Commute,
9 a.m.	School	School	School	School	School	Job	Church
	School	School	School	School	School	Job	Church
10 a.m.	School	School	School	School	School	Job	Church
	School	School	School	School	School	Job	Church
11 a.m.	School	School	School	School	School	Job	Commute,
	School	School	School	School	School	Job	Chores
Noon	School	School	School	School	School	Job	Chores
	Eat	Eat	Eat	Eat	Eat	Commute,	Chores
1 p.m.	School	School	School	School	School	Sports	Chores
	School	School	School	School	School	Sports	Eat
2 p.m.	School	School	School	School	School	Sports	Eat
	School	School	School	School	School	Sports	Eat
3 p.m.	Sports	Sports	Sports	Sports	Sports	Sports	Eat
	Sports	Sports	Sports	Sports	Sports	Sports	Eat

Practice

Modify the "TimePlan" spreadsheet to match your schedule for a typical school week. If you are between semesters or quarters, you may not know which courses you'll have on which days and at what time. So, make up a possible schedule and rearrange it when school starts. If you do not know what courses you'll take, make some reasonable assumptions.

Schedule your time in blocks of 30 minutes. Schedule time for sleep, dressing, eating and commuting. Include the time you spend watching TV, talking on the telephone, or just hanging out with friends.

Feedback

Once you have entered your schedule for a typical week, note that the hours for each day's activities add up to 24. There are 168 hours in a week. (24 hours per day times 7 days per week = 168 hours per week.)

How Do You Want to Spend Your Time?

Now that you know more about how you are spending your time, consider how to make time a friendlier ally in reaching your goals. Here are some guidelines for planning time in new ways:

1. **Set realistic goals and schedules.** Scheduling your time is a tradeoff between school, job, social life, hobbies, school events, sports, etc. You may be busier now than you have ever been. Being realistic about your time commitments is an act of kindness to yourself.

2. **Adjust your schedule to match your goals.**

3. **Allow adequate time to sleep every night.**

4. **Schedule 2 hours of study time for every hour you spend in class.** If you must fill in any gaps in what you should already know, add extra time for that.

5. **Avoid marathon study sessions.** Doing your Spanish an hour a day for a week is usually easier and more effective than doing six hours of Spanish on Sunday. When you schedule yourself for a six-hour marathon, it is hard to stay focused and efficient.

6. **Schedule time for fun.**

7. **Allow flexibility in your schedule for unexpected things.**

8. **Plan to plan.** Schedule time for scheduling your week.

Practice

Following the guidelines above, revise your weekly schedule to better use the time you have. In doing this, consider these questions:

1. Have I planned to do what I want, need, or agreed to do?
2. Am I doing something to avoid doing something else?
3. Am I planning to do this task well enough or perhaps too well?
4. Should I be doing something else?

Feedback

Before going on, discuss your schedule with your professor.

The Tools of Time Management

Keeping track of things you must do is essential for success in school and everywhere else. Keep a To-Do List. You can do this with an app on your smartphone or laptop. Or use a printed datebook or planner. Whatever you choose should be portable so that you can always have your To-Do List with you. Add new items as they come up. And check off items as you complete them. Those checks are a visible sign that you're getting things done—one of the great pleasures in keeping a To-Do List.

If you have kept a To-Do List or Assignment Log or Calendar in the past, you have probably experienced problems like these. First, the list quickly gets long and scary. Second, some tasks take so long that you can only to a portion on any day. So, when do you schedule it? Finally, since you never run out of things you need or want to do, you may feel like you are not making any progress, which is discouraging.

Here's an approach that is likely to be more effective and satisfying. Limit your To-Do List to just the things you can and will do today. If you can only do a portion of some tasks in the time available today, list the part you plan to complete. Make estimates of how long various tasks will take and don't overload yourself. You may rarely finish everything you plan to do, but with a little experience, you are likely to complete 80% or 90% of your daily To-Dos. You are likely to get more done every day and to feel more in control. Create your Daily To-Do List either the night before or first thing in the morning.

In addition to your Daily To-Do List, you will probably find it helpful to keep a log of all the current and future assignments and tasks that you need to. This log will help you remember assignments and due dates. When you plan to do a smallish task, you transfer it to your Daily To-Do List. For bigger tasks, you probably will want to break it into pieces that you will do on different days.

So, now you've got a Weekly TimePlan, a Daily To-Do List, a log of assignments with due dates, and a calendar for appointments and events. These are the tools of time management. With these tools, you are likely to get more done and to feel relaxed and in control of your life. Without them, well, you probably know how that feels.

Practice

Write your To-Do List for today and tomorrow.

Time
Estimate Item

_____ _____

_____ _____

_____ _____

_____ _____

_____ _____

_____ _____

_____ _____

_____ _____

_____ _____

Once you have your list and time estimates, compare the total time to your available time. If you think you can get something more done, add it to the list. More likely, if you have more to do than you have time for, take lower priority items off the list. Figure out what you are not going to do and scratch it out. Try to be a good manager of your time and your life. Don't be too easy on yourself. But don't be unreasonable, either. Give yourself a challenging but doable workload each day. Enjoy the feeling of creating your future and taking charge of your life—now.

Mastery Criteria

To check that you have mastered this lesson, show these items to your professor and discuss them together:

- Your weekly TimePlan, adjusted to allocate your time in the way you think will work best for you.
- Your To-Do List for today and tomorrow
- A log of future assignments and tasks, with due dates.
- Your calendar.

Lesson 3

The Right Kinds of Practice

You already know that we emphasize learning by doing. We find that most of anyone's learning occurs when they practice doing what they are learning to do. In college classes, you usually get little or no practice. Even if you actively participate in a discussion, you are likely to be speaking only a few minutes per hour. In comparison, two to three hours of studying is 10 to 15 times as much practice. That is why practicing and learning outside of class is critical to your success in college.

Practice

Write a few words or sentences to describe the way you feel about studying and your approach to doing it. Are there subjects or study activities that you like or dislike? Do you practice to mastery? When you get stuck understanding something or doing a problem, what do you do?

_____

_____

_____

Planning to Learn Your Assignments

Professors often give assignments like this: "Read Chapter 3." If you do the reading, you will understand and remember some of what is in Chapter 3. But you are unlikely to have mastered that material and to remember it in a week.

Don't be fooled by the assignment. The professor fully intends for you to do more than just read the chapter. She wants you to master the material. That means you can explain it, answer questions about it, and apply it. Just reading the chapter, even if you highlight key ideas, and even if you read it twice, won't get you there. To be able to do those things, you will have to practice explaining and answering questions, orally or in writing, to yourself or someone else.

At this point, you may be wondering where you are going to find the time for that extra practice. Surely, that will take you longer than just reading the chapter. But, let me repeat. The extra time investment pays off because your learning rate increases. So, you save time on all your future assignments and studying for tests. You will wind up spending less time to get A's than it would have taken to get C's by just reading and highlighting. In this course, you will try this and see how well it works.

When you sit down to study a lesson in any course, take a minute or so to plan your approach. We have provided a "LearningPlan" form to help you get started doing this. Once you get the idea, you can continue to use the LearningPlan form or not, as you choose.

The usual Assignment Sheet or Student Planner calls for:

- Due date
- Assignment—for example, "Read Chapter 3."

A LearningPlan also asks for:

- What are you supposed to learn?
Example: Solve word problems involving distances, speeds and times.

- What instruction will you get to prepare to practice?
Example: Watch a video, read a chapter in your textbook, or listen in class.

- How will you practice?
Example: Solve problems at the end of the section in the book.

- How will you get help and feedback while practicing?
Example: Call or text a classmate.

The kind of practice depends on what you are learning to do. Examples are:

- Answer the questions on a test.
- Discuss the ideas orally.
- Use the facts and methods to solve problems.

Practice

Follow these directions to open the online LearningPlan form.

LearningPlan Spreadsheet

You will use the LearningPlan spreadsheet for this exercise. Here are directions for two ways to download the spreadsheet from the Internet.

Recommended Method: Use a Google Account

- If you have Gmail, you already have a Google Account. If not, sign up for a free Google Account at https://accounts.google.com/SignUp?hl=en
- Sign in to Google Drive at www.Drive.Google.com using your Gmail address and password.
- In a new browser window, go to this URL:

    https://goo.gl/MdSZ42

The LearningPlan will open as a View only file.

- Click on the File menu at the upper left and select Add to My Drive. You will now have an editable copy of LearningPlan in Drive.

Alternative Method: Download to your own computer

- In a browser window, enter this URL: https://goo.gl/MdSZ42 The TimePlan will open as a View only file.
- Download the file to a folder on your computer as an xlsx file.
- To open, edit and save your LearningPlan.xlsx. Use a spreadsheet program such as Microsoft EXCEL or the Google Drive app.

Feedback

The LearningPlan looks like this:

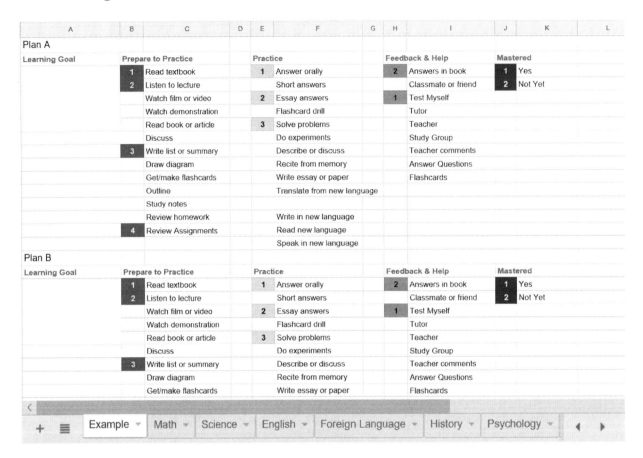

Using the LearningPlan Spreadsheet

The LearningPlan has tabs for different worksheets for various subjects. There are somewhat different choices for each subject. In addition, you can add or change entries to meet your needs.

You can make copies of a worksheet by right-clicking a tab and selecting Duplicate. You can rename a worksheet by double-clicking a tab and typing a new name.

Each worksheet has room for four plans, labeled A, B, C and D. You can use these to create plans for the various types of assignments you may get in that subject.

Practice

On your copy of the LearningPlan spreadsheet, duplicate one of the worksheets. Rename the new worksheet with any course name. Enter a number or x next to a few entries for Prepare to Practice, Practice, and Help & Feedback. Save your spreadsheet.

Feedback

If you need help, ask your professor or a classmate.

Practice

Duplicate the Math worksheet and name the new worksheet "Algebra." On the new sheet, create a plan for mastering this Algebra assignment. Don't do the assignment. Just plan how you would proceed to learn it.

> **Assignment:** Learn to draw and explain the number line by reading sections 1.1 and 1.2 of Chapter 1 of the textbook. Do the first six problems on page 12.

Feedback

Plan A								
Learning Goal		**Prepare to Practice**		**Practice**		**Feedback & Help**		**Mastered**
Draw, explain and solve problems using the number line.	1	Read textbook		Answer orally		1	Answers in book	1	Yes
		Listen to lecture		Short answers		Classmate or friend		Not Yet
		Watch film or video		Essay answers	2	Test Myself		
		Watch demonstration		Flashcard drill		Tutor		
		Read book or article	1	Solve problems		Teacher		
		Discuss		Do experiments		Study Group		
		Write list or summary	2	Describe or discuss		Teacher comments		
	2	Draw diagram		Recite from memory		Answers to Questions		
		Get/make flashcards		Write essay or paper		Flashcards		
		Outline		Translate to new language				
		Study notes		Translate from new language				
		Review homework		Write in new language				
		Review Assignments		Read new language				
				Speak in new language				
Plan B								

‹ › | Example | Math | **Algebra** | Science | English | Foreign Language | History | Psych ... ⊕ ⋮ ◀

Practice

1. At what stage in your LearningPlan would you have completed your preparation and be ready to start practicing?
    *   When you sit down to begin this assignment.
    *   When you begin reading Sections 1.1 and 1.2.
    *   When you have read Sections 1.1 and 1.2.
    *   When you have mastered the assignment.

2. You have completed practicing when you have:
    *   Done the six problems.
    *   Done the six problems correctly.
    *   Mastered the material.
    *   Something else.

3. Assume there are answers to just the odd-numbered problems at the back of the textbook. Which of the following are ways you could get feedback on your work? Check all that apply.
    *   Check odd problems against answers in the book.
    *   Check even problems yourself, by working the problems backward.
    *   Ask a classmate or friend who is good at algebra to check your work.
    *   Wait for the professor to correct and return the homework.
    *   See the professor during a conference hour and ask her to review your work.

4. After practicing and getting feedback, you may not feel you have mastered the material. If not, which of the following might you do? Check all that apply.
    *   Re-read Sections 1.1 and 1.2.
    *   Call a classmate to discuss the material.
    *   Work additional problems on page 12.
    *   Work additional problems from another book.
    *   Makeup and solve additional problems of your own.
    *   Ask the professor for additional problems and solve them.

Feedback

1. At what stage would you have completed your preparation and be ready to start practicing?
   - When you sit down to begin this assignment.
   - When you begin reading Sections 1.1 and 1.2.
   - **When you have read Sections 1.1 and 1.2.**
   - When you have mastered the assignment.

2. You have completed practicing when you have:
   - Done the six problems.
   - Done the six problems correctly.
   - **Mastered the material.**
   - Something else.

3. Assume there are answers to just the odd-numbered problems at the back of the textbook. Which of the following are ways you could get feedback on your work? Check all that apply.
   - **Check odd problems against answers in the book.**
   - **Check even problems yourself, by working the problems backward.**
   - **Ask a classmate or friend who is good at algebra to check your work.**
   - **Wait for the professor to correct and return the homework.**
   - **See the professor during a conference hour and ask her to review your work.**

4. After practicing and getting feedback, you may not feel you have mastered the material. If not, which of the following might you do? Check all that apply.
   - **Re-read Sections 1.1 and 1.2.**
   - **Call a classmate to discuss the material.**
   - **Work additional problems on page 12.**
   - **Work additional problems from another book.**
   - **Makeup and solve additional problems of your own.**
   - **Ask the professor for additional problems and solve them.**

Note: Re-reading the textbook is usually the weakest way to achieve mastery.

3 General Types of Practice

The key to learning is to practice to mastery. Now it's time to look more closely at the best kinds of practice for various types of content.

Begin with three general types of practice:

- Memorizing
- Performing
- Solving

Many college courses involve memorizing basic facts, dates, names, words, formulas, and concepts. This type of information provides a base for later learning. Some examples of things you learn by memorizing are:

- Number of days in each month, and in a year
- Multiplication tables
- Names of parts of the body
- Vocabulary and spelling
- Names and locations of states, countries, continents, etc.
- Historical dates, people, and events

The second type of practice is performing. Examples are:

- Writing a story
- Taking a test
- Speaking a foreign language
- Public speaking
- Typing

You can memorize facts about such activities, but that will take you only so far. Performing calls for doing—taking some action beyond learning information or ideas. Suppose, for example, that you want to get better at writing analytical essays about government. It will help to read some sample essays in magazines and to listen to a lecture on essay writing. But, the most powerful way to learn this skill is to write essays.

Finally, you can practice by solving problems. For example:

- Doing story problems in math
- Writing a book report
- Discussing a current event
- Analyzing an experiment in science

Practice

Pick the most appropriate approach (memorizing, performing, or problem-solving) for each of the following learning tasks:

1. Write the Declaration of Independence without reference to books or notes.

Type of practice:

      memorizing   performing   problem-solving

2. Calculate how much money you will earn on your job in the next month.

Type of practice:

      memorizing   performing   problem-solving

3. Draw a cartoon character.

Type of practice:

      memorizing   performing   problem-solving

Feedback

1. Write the Declaration of Independence without reference to books or notes.

Type of practice:

      memorizing   performing   problem-solving

2. Calculate how much money you will earn on your job in the next month.

Type of practice:

      memorizing   performing   **problem-solving**

3. Draw a cartoon character.

Type of practice:

      memorizing   **performing**   problem-solving

Practice

1. List the three main types of practice. Then give one or two examples of each one.

2. For any course in college, you'll probably want to use:

- Just one type of practice.
- Several types of practice equally.
- Several types of practice, but maybe one more than the others.

3. What is the main approach you'll probably use for the usual courses in each of these areas?

Math:
Foreign language:
Astronomy:

Feedback

1. List the three main types of practice. Then give one or two examples of each one.

- Memorizing: Vocabulary, dates, facts, names.
- Performing: Spelling, speaking and understanding a foreign language, using a microscope, creative writing.
- Problem-solving: Math problems, recommend solutions to traffic congestion.

2. For any course in college, you'll probably want to use:

- Just one type of practice.
- Several types of practice equally.
- **Several types of practice, but maybe one more than the others.**

3. What is the type of practice you'll probably use most for the usual courses in each of these areas?

Math: Problem-solving
Foreign language: Performing
Astronomy: Memorizing

Practice

For a typical assignment in one of the other courses you are currently taking, fill out a LearningPlan in the LearningPlan spreadsheet, to answer these questions.

- What are you supposed to learn?
Example: Solve word problems involving distances, speeds and times.

- What instruction will you get to prepare to practice?
Example: Watch a video, read a chapter in your textbook, or listen in class.

- How will you practice?
Example: Solve problems at the end of the section in the book.

- How will you get help and feedback while practicing?
Example: Call or text a classmate.

Feedback

If you have any questions about creating a LearningPlan, ask your professor or a classmate for help. When you are comfortable that you have the idea, go to the next practice.

Practice

For typical assignments in each of your other courses, fill out a LearningPlan.

Compare each of your LearningPlans to how you have been studying in those courses.

Mastery Criteria

Your professor will discuss your LearningPlans with you.

Lesson 4

Memorize and Remember

Memorizing is one of the most common tasks students face. If remembering names, dates and concepts has been a pain for you in the past, relax. There's probably nothing wrong with your memory. You may just need some better ways to get stuff into your head, so it stays there and is easier to recall later.

You've got about two pounds of gray matter in your head with more power than a supercomputer. The methods you will learn in this lesson will help you get that supercomputer brain of yours into gear to help you.

Learning by Listening and Watching

Look/Look Away: A Good Way to Memorize

Use Reviewing for Long-Term Memories

Consider the Costs of Cramming

Memory by Association

Pictures and Pindar's Trick

Flashcards: Flexible, Faithful, and Forgiving

Learning by Listening and Watching

Often, we don't do anything special to store things in memory or pull them out again. For instance, you go to a movie and watch it without conscious effort. During that time, your mind is storing information—images and sounds. Then a friend asks you about the movie, and you can describe it. This works well for movies, but not so well for the unfamiliar information you must learn in college.

Usually, it is not enough to listen, watch and read. That misses a critical ingredient for learning: active practice.

Practice

The methods I currently use to memorize material include....

_____

_____

_____

How do you usually memorize? How well has that worked for you?

_____

_____

_____

I think learning some new memory techniques might provide me with these benefits:

_____

_____

_____

Look/Look Away: A Good Way to Memorize

Many memory techniques are just ways to make sure your brain is going over information again and again. For example, there's a simple way to learn a friend's telephone number or the words to a song: keep repeating the number or the words until you can recall them at will.

When memorizing a small amount of information, you may find this technique alone does the trick. Other techniques in this lesson are useful when you have lots more to remember.

Let's go back to memorizing phone numbers for a minute. When repeating a number to yourself, you're using an effective memory principle—even if you don't realize it. Let's say you look up a phone number online and say it once or twice. Then you look away and say it a few more times to be sure you have it. You are practicing putting the information in and getting it back.

On the other hand, if you just read the number aloud, even four or five times, you may not remember it as well. That's because you are not practicing remembering. You are reading rather than pulling the number from memory. Once again, we're back to practice as the key to learning.

Check out the illustration on this page. When you want to memorize something, look at the material. Then look away and say it. If you get stuck, glance down for a reminder. Then look up and recite again. This technique is called the look/look away method.

You can talk about eight times faster than you can write. Since most of us need about the same number of repetitions to memorize something by reciting or writing, reciting can save you lots of time.

Here's another hint. Some people find it easier to memorize while walking. Experiment with pacing or walking around as you memorize.

To memorize something word-for-word, master one phrase or sentence at a time. Completely master the first portion before working on the second. Mastery means you can say it without straining or stumbling—as fast as spelling your name. After you master the second sentence, master the first and second sentences together before working on the third. Continue in that way until you have memorized the material.

Practice: Look/Look Away

This exercise is to memorize a passage from Shakespeare, using the look/look away technique. You might master this assignment in less than one hour, or it might take somewhat longer. Here are some suggestions on how to proceed:

- Read the whole passage. Several unusual words are defined below. Look up any other words you don't know in a dictionary.
- Notice that the passage is organized based on the stages of life.
- Use the look/look away method to memorize the first line, then the second. Next, master the first two lines of the poem together before starting on line three. Proceed through the rest of the passage in the same way.
- When you start to work on each sentence, create a picture in your mind to go with that sentence.
- Notice that as you learn the words, the poetry begins to make more sense. Notice also how it feels to master an assignment like this.

Master this passage as though you were memorizing a part for a play or the words to a song. Aim to get every word exactly right, and to recite the whole piece without stumbling or pausing to think.

When you're done memorizing the passage, ask your professor to listen as you recite, and to judge whether you have learned the method and used it to the master the script.

DEFINITIONS OF UNUSUAL WORDS

capon: a neutered rooster

hose: long stockings

mewling: babbling

pantaloon: pants

pard: a character in Chaucer's Canterbury Tales, who even as an adult man had only "peach fuzz" rather than a beard.

sans: without

saws: sayings

shank: body or legs

woeful: sad

Passage from *As You Like It* by William Shakespeare

(This famous quotation is from a speech by Jacques.)

All the world's a stage,
And all the men and women merely players.
They have their exits and their entrances;
And one man in his time plays many parts,
His acts being seven ages. As first the infant,
Mewling and puking in the nurse's arms.
And then the whining schoolboy, with his satchel,
And shining morning face, creeping like snail
Unwillingly to school, And then the lover,
Sighing like furnace, with a woeful ballad
Made to his mistress' eyebrow. Then the soldier,
Full of strange oaths, and bearded like the pard,
Jealous in honor, sudden and quick in quarrel,
Seeking the bubble reputation
Even in the cannon's mouth.

And then the justice,
In fair round belly with good capon lined,
With eyes severe and beard of formal cut,
Full of wise saws and modern instances,
And so he plays his part. The sixth age shifts
Into the lean and slipper'd pantaloon,
With spectacles on nose and pouch on side;
His youthful hose, well saved a world too wide
For his shrunk shank; and his big manly voice,
Turning again toward childish treble, pipes
And whistles in his sound. Last scene of all,
That ends this strange eventful history,
Is second childishness, and mere oblivion,
Sans teeth, sans eyes, sans taste, sans everything.

Use Reviewing for Long-Term Memories

When you memorize a telephone number, you might recite that number a few times. That way, you remember the number well enough to dial. This works great when you want to store something in short-term memory. If you want to remember that number weeks or months later, then you will need reviews to move the information from short-term memory to long-term memory.

Suppose it takes you ten repetitions to learn the words to a new song. If you repeat the song 15 times today, you may remember more of it next week than if you only repeated it ten times. This is called over-learning. But there's a better way.

Instead of over-learning, use reviews spread over time. You start with look/look away to master the words. Then take a five- or ten-minute break. Review until you again have the song mastered. Repeat the process the next day. If you want to remember the song for a month, you will probably need another review next week.

When you use reviews over time, prepare for an exciting discovery: Reviewing soon after learning and again the next day can be far more effective than putting in the same amount of work all at once.

To experience this benefit when you study, apply the following steps:

- Practice to mastery.
- Break for 5 to 10 minutes
- Do your first review (practice to mastery)
- Review the next day (practice to mastery)
- Review next week (practice to mastery)
- Review next month (practice to mastery)

The times in this plan are approximate.

Practice

Several days have probably passed since you memorized the Power Learner Mindset in Lesson 1. Review the six statements now. If you stumble, use the look/look away method to bring yourself back to mastery. As before, master each sentence in turn, and then master it with those you have already mastered.

Review again within 24 hours.

Consider the Costs of Cramming

Cramming is studying intensely right before a test. That may work well enough for you to pass a test. But cramming ignores the need for spaced reviews to put information into long-term memory. Consequently, most people rapidly forget after they cram. And forgetting means that they do not build up the storehouse of knowledge that will increase your learning rate on subsequent assignments.

In summary, here are some pros and cons of cramming:

Pros:

- You may be able to learn enough in the time available.
- You might pass the exam at the last minute.

Cons:

- Forgetting what you have already learned in a course slows you down. The course will likely become increasingly difficult, annoying, and discouraging.
- You don't remember as much of the material for future use. So, you fail to build a foundation for later learning.
- The experience of not understanding the subject and of forgetting information can have a negative impact on your self-esteem and energy level.

If you do end up cramming, there's no reason to get down on yourself. Instead, forgive yourself and decide to start practicing and reviewing so you won't need cramming next time.

Practice

Indicate whether each of the following is true or false:

Cramming doesn't work. You'll forget everything during the test.
       T   F
One problem with cramming is that you quickly forget what you learned.
       T   F
A penalty of cramming is that you don't build up your storehouse of information for associations and mental pictures that make later learning easier.
       T   F

Feedback

Cramming doesn't work. You'll forget everything during the test.
          T   **F**
One problem with cramming is that you quickly forget what you learned.
          T   F
A penalty of cramming is that you don't build up your storehouse of information for associations and mental pictures that make later learning easier.
          T   F

Some Memory by Association Tricks that Sometimes Help

Repetition and review are the primary ways to record information in your memory. Adding another technique—association—can make memorizing easier and more fun. Here are some tips that you may find helpful.

Connect the material to your interests

We tend to remember material that aligns with our interests. If the subject you're learning seems outside your interests, then search for an interesting connection. For example, perhaps you can relate American history to the development of jazz and rock music. Someone who loves cars can connect several areas in physics to automobiles.

Go for understanding

It's usually easier to remember material that you understand. It's easier for a baseball fan to remember the scores of today's games than it is for someone who doesn't know the difference between home plate and a home run. So, before you start to memorize something, do whatever it takes for you to understand it: Talk to another student. See your professor. Review the material with a parent or family member. Know what problem this material helps you solve and ask how you would apply this material outside of class. Go for the big picture. Understand the rules before the exceptions. Organize the material by outlining or drawing a mind map. Understanding is especially important in math and science, where it's easy to confuse formulas and how to apply them.

Use mnemonics

This word is pronounced as though it were spelled "nemonics," without the first m. A mnemonic is a play on words that helps you to remember something. The following jingles offer examples: Thirty days have September, April, June, and November. All the rest have 31, except February. Here's another mnemonic: "i" before "e" except after "c," or when sounded like "a" as in "neighbor" and "weigh." Mnemonics are sometimes helpful, but repetition, with understanding and connection to your interests, is usually more effective.

Use acronyms

An acronym is a word formed by the first letters in a series of other words. For example, NASA is an acronym for the National Aeronautics and Space Administration. Another acronym is the word HOMES, used to remember the names of the Great Lakes: Huron, Ontario, Michigan, Erie, and Superior. Like mnemonics, acronyms are sometimes helpful, but often more trouble than they are worth.

Picture This

Using pictures to learn and remember is another playful yet effective technique. The parts of the brain that process verbal information also handle logic, numbers, and words. Other parts of the brain excel in recognizing patterns and remembering images. To draw on your full brain power, form a picture to go with the words.

Certain subjects—such as literature, history, and science—lend themselves well to mental pictures. Say that you're reading the *Autobiography of Malcolm X*. In your mind, enter the author's world. See Malcolm X in the library at Norfolk Prison Colony, seeking to improve his vocabulary by copying the dictionary word-for-word. Or, create pictures in biology. As you learn the difference between smooth muscle and skeletal muscle, picture the different parts of the human body where these muscles are located.

In some cases, the material doesn't suggest any image. For instance, reading about the importance of private property in capitalism may not bring any picture to your mind. Be creative; the picture doesn't have to make sense. Perhaps you could visualize the man with the top hat shown on Monopoly Chance Cards. See him walking down the street clutching stacks of hotels and houses—a capitalist holding his private property.

That's corny, but it may help.

Here's an example of using your image artistry. Think of the name of any state in the United States that is on the east coast. Now name one that is on the west coast. Finally, name a state that is near the middle of the country. If you did these mini-exercises, you probably pictured a map of the United States. This is an example of using pictures as a memory aid.

Both exercises above help demonstrate that you already use pictures to remember things. Knowing this, you might decide to make wider use of this technique.

Pindar's Trick

One of the most famous and commonly used methods of memorizing using pictures is called Pindar's Trick. It is named for the Greek poet Pindar, who lived over 2,000 years ago, and whose poetry was difficult to remember. To get the hang of this technique, read the description of Pindar's Trick below. Then do the exercises on the pages that follow.

Begin by memorizing a list of numbered words. Choose words that bring to mind clear images and rhyme with the numbers one to ten. A common example is:

1. bun   4. door   7. heaven   10. hen
2. shoe 5. Hive   8. gate
3. tree 6. sticks 9. pine

Whatever list you choose, plan to use it permanently.

Then, whenever you want to remember a list of items, in your mind's eye, imagine a picture of each item in combination with the next image and number from your "Pindar" list. Suppose you have three errands to run: pick up your jacket at the cleaners, buy a quart of milk, and buy a newspaper. You could create these associations:

1. *One, bun, jacket at cleaners:* Picture a bun in the pocket of your jacket.
2. *Two, shoe, milk:* Picture pouring milk into a shoe.
3. *Three, tree, newspaper:* Picture newspapers hanging like fruit on a tree.

Note that the associations don't have to make sense. In fact, silly or graphic associations are often easier to recall. Each time you have a new list of items to remember, create a new set of associations using your permanent "Pindar list."

Pindar's Trick is handy for a small number of items, say, up to 20. For items 11 through 20, you can use your permanent Pindar list over again starting with 1. There are memory experts who give demonstrations and compete in contests. These experts use Pindar lists of 100 items or more.

Pindar's trick is especially helpful when memorizing items in a specific order. For example, you might have to learn the order in which the original 13 colonies ratified the U.S. Constitution or the names of U.S. presidents in order.

Like other memory techniques, Pindar's Trick has limitations. Don't expect it to work for all subjects, all the time. But, in some cases, you might find it almost magical. Try using it in the following practice.

Practice

1.   Memorize a permanent list of items that rhyme with the numbers from 1 to 10.

2.   Use Pindar's Trick and your permanent list to memorize the ten largest cities in the United States, listed below in the order of population. Do not memorize by repetition. Form a mental picture that associates each city with the corresponding item from your permanent Pindar's list.

   1. New York City, NY. Population: 8,550,405. ...
   2. Los Angeles, CA. Population: 3,971,883. ...
   3. Chicago, IL. Population: 2,720,546. ...
   4. Houston, TX. Population: 2,296,224. ...
   5. Philadelphia, PA. Population: 1,567,442. ...
   6. Phoenix, AZ. Population: 1,563,025. ...
   7. San Antonio, TX. Population: 1,469,845. ...
   8. San Diego, CA. Population: 1,394,928.
   9. Dallas, TX
   10. San Jose, CA

3. Take a short break and test yourself. See if you can name the fifth largest city, or the eighth largest city, without counting through the list.

Feedback

When you've finished this lesson, your professor may ask you to list these cities and to describe the picture you created to associate each city with an item on your permanent Pindar's list.

Flashcards

Flashcards are not kid-stuff. When you make and use flashcards, you automatically apply many aspects of mastery learning, including preparation, practice, and feedback. Once you have the flashcards, they can make reviewing and preparing for exams a snap. Investing a few minutes in creating flashcards can save you hours in the long run.

Flashcards are particularly useful in school when you must learn facts such as:

- Names, dates, events in history
- Meanings of words
- Scientific facts and theories
- Vocabulary in a foreign language
- Mathematical formulas and facts
- Rules of grammar

In addition, flashcards have many admirable qualities. They never sleep, so they're available to you 24 hours each day. They never complain about being used over and over again. They never scold you for a wrong answer. And once you are done with them, you can use flashcards as bookmarks, coasters, fireplace starters, and guitar picks. All told, flashcards are some of the most flexible, faithful, and forgiving teachers you'll ever find.

You can make flashcards on index cards or paper, but flashcard software is very convenient for these reasons:

- It is faster to type out an electronic flashcard than to write on cards.
- Most software makes it easy to drill and learn, repeating any cards you miss automatically.
- You can share your electronic flashcards with others and use flashcards created by others.

There are many flashcard programs available, some of which are free. One that we like is available at **http://ankisrs.net/** This program works on Microsoft Windows, Mac, and Linux computers. It's free, though the author requests that you donate to support the program.

Here are a few suggestions for drilling with flashcards.

- If you have a lot of flashcards to learn at one time, work with no more than 25 at a time. Master the first 25. Next, master the second 25. Then combine them and master all 50 of those combined before taking the next set of 25 cards.
- Shuffle the deck from time to time.
- Review the cards the next day and again within the next week.

Spelling—Don't use flashcards to learn to spell. When you look at the word on a flashcard, you see the "answer" right away. That prompting slows your learning. Instead, get a friend or classmate to quiz you orally. Or record the words yourself. Then play back the words and spell them.

Word-for-word memorizing—When memorizing a list such as the six statements of the Power Learner Mindset (page 13), you may find it easier to refer to the original text than to recopy it on flashcards.

Sketch and label diagrams—In some courses you might have to sketch a map and label cities, rivers, and other geographic features. For other courses, such as biology, you may learn the names of parts of plants and animals. In these cases, your learning involves a sketch or diagram. Here it makes sense to practice directly with that chart or diagram instead of a flashcard.

If the professor gives you a worksheet or a diagram to label the parts of something, make a couple of photocopies to use when you review for tests. Making copies is easier than creating flashcards.

Practice

Create a set of flashcards covering the techniques discussed in this lesson. (They're listed below.) This is not a test. Feel free to look back through the lesson to refresh your memory.

- Look/Look Away
- Review to Mastery
- Associations: Interest, understanding, mnemonics, acronyms
- Pictures and Pindar's Trick
- Flashcards

Write the name of each technique on a single card. On the back of each card, describe the technique and give one or more examples of when you might use it.

Drill with your flashcards until you feel sure you will remember these techniques. Tomorrow, review using these flashcards again.

Mastery Criteria

Demonstrate your mastery of the techniques in this lesson to your professor:

- Recite the passage from Shakespeare.
- Recite the six statements of the Power Learner Mindset.
- Use Pindar's Trick to list the ten largest cities in the United States, in order of size. Your professor will ask you to describe the pictures you created to associate the cities with images on your permanent Pindar's list.
- Describe the techniques for learning and remembering the techniques that you learned in this lesson.

Lesson 5

Get More as You Read and Listen

Has this ever happened to you? You read a page in a textbook and realize you don't remember one thing from that page. Ever walk out of school at the end of the day and realize that you can't remember one thing that your teachers presented? When these things happen, do you worry about your ability to concentrate or remember? The overwhelming odds are that your mind is fine. You just aren't using effective methods. Methods you will learn in this lesson.

Preparing to Practice

It's as Simple as PRQT

Taking Notes: Main Ideas and Key Facts

Taking Notes: Outlining

Taking Notes: Mind Mapping

Receiving Information

As you now know, we divide earning into three main steps: getting information to prepare to practice, then learning by practicing, and getting feedback on your progress. Research indicates that practice is key. But maybe you, like many students, have mistakenly thought that you are supposed to understand and remember new information just by hearing it or reading it once. That is never going to happen for most of us. Still, the more you can get from reading, watching and listening, the better.

IT'S AS SIMPLE AS PRQT

We begin with reading. One method you can use every time you read a textbook is called PRQT. The initials stand for:

PREVIEW

READ & QUESTION

TEST

To apply this method, study the definitions on the next few pages until you understand each step well enough to do it.

Preview

Just sitting down and starting to slog through the text once, from beginning to end, is not the best way to learn from a textbook. Whether reading a whole book or a chapter, start by looking it over. Get a sense of what it's about, how it's organized, and how long it is. Read the first paragraph or first page. Read the last paragraph or last page. Scan charts, tables, and pictures.

Read headings and titles. You might also read just the first sentence of each paragraph as a preview.

If your professor has given you review or study questions, read those as part of your preview. And if there are questions at the end of the chapter, as in many textbooks, read those too. Reading the questions before reading the chapter is a guide to the information the author and your professor intend for you to learn.

Read and Question

Read the material one paragraph at a time. At the end of each paragraph, write at least one flashcard about the material in that paragraph. Create your flashcards on 3x5 index cards or using a flashcard program, as described below. Below the answer on the flashcard, write the page number and the paragraph number, so you will know where you found the information. The first paragraph on each page is #1; the second is #2, and so on.

Some paragraphs have enough information for two or more questions. If so, write questions to cover everything that you want to know. Write each question on a separate flashcard, with the answer on the back.

Reading this way may seem like a lot of work, especially when compared to just highlighting the key facts. But there's a reward for your effort. You will be able to use your flashcards to master the material quickly and to review for tests. That will save you time compared to re-reading the text, and you will get better results.

Highlighting seems easy, and many students do it. But highlighting merely marks information you need to learn. You still must learn it by doing something that engraves the information into your memory, such as drilling with flashcards.

Test

When you've finished reading and questioning, drill with your deck of flashcards. Put the questions you answer correctly in a pile to your right. Get it? The "right" ones go on the right. Put those you miss in a pile to your left. Keep working on the cards until they're all on your right. Then shuffle and go through the whole stack again. Continue until you have mastered these questions.

By this time, you'll be prepared to answer any questions you were assigned.

Here are some of the advantages people have reported after using PRQT:

- *You learn more with this method.*
- *PRQT takes more time than just reading, but less time to learn the material.*
- *PRQT reduces study time for tests. You can practice with flashcards instead of re-reading the chapters.*
- *With PRQT, you are less likely to get bored or confused.*

Practice

To be sure you remember the PRQT method, list the PRQT steps and a short description of each step on a 3x5 index card. Use this as a bookmark and quick reference card while you read.

Use PRQT for one of your next reading assignments. If you don't have a current reading assignment, practice PRQT on a chapter in one of your textbooks.

Feedback

Consider how well the PRQT method worked for you. Keep in mind that any technique might feel awkward when you first use it.

Practice

Complete the following sentences.

In the past, I typically had these reactions to textbook reading assignments:

_____

_____

_____

While using PRQT, I had these reactions:

_____

_____

Reading Faster and Understanding Better

In addition to better methods for studying a textbook, you can also learn more in less time by increasing your reading skills. In this section, you will first measure how fast you read and then how well you understand what you read. Finally, you can consider investing some time to increase your speed and comprehension.

Measuring Your Reading Rate

Your reading rate is how many words you can read in a minute. This rate will vary with the material you are reading. It also depends on how thoroughly you must read to get the information you need from a book or article.

Without knowing their reading rate, many people consider themselves slow readers. You might as well find out. If your reading rate is slow, then your school assignments may take too much time. Luckily, slow readers can probably double their reading speed with just a few hours of practice. As slow readers practice reading faster, they often understand and remember more. So, faster reading can not only save you time but help you learn more as well.

Practice

Time yourself reading the 512-word essay on the next two pages. Read at your usual rate, without daydreaming or rushing. Just read at the rate you normally use for school material. Use a stopwatch to time yourself. There are some free stopwatches available online, such as the one at **http://www.online-stopwatch.com/full-screen-stopwatch/**

512 Word Essay for Reading Speed Test

Suggestions for Better Tutoring

During a tutoring session, the student is the client. If you are tutoring your son or daughter, it may seem strange to think of him or her as your client. After all, as the parent, you are in charge. But if you want to be an effective tutor, you must serve the client, even if he is your child and isn't paying you.

Similarly, if you are considering hiring a tutor for your teen, ask the tutor about his style. And after you hire a tutor, when you observe him with your teen, or when you talk to the tutor or your teen, consider this issue. Your teen will benefit most from tutoring that addresses his concerns. If the tutor is too controlling, your teen may feel that the tutoring is like adding another course to his workload.

So, any tutor—whether it is you or a hired tutor—should let the student determine:

- What he wants to work on
- When he wants a demonstration or explanation of how to do something
- When he wants a question answered or an answer repeated or rephrased
- When he wants another problem of the same difficulty, a harder one, or an easier one
- When he wants to keep thinking or working on a problem.
- When he wants feedback
- How and when he wants to be quizzed or tested

Sometimes the student doesn't know what he should work on next. So, he should say to the tutor: "I really don't know how to attack this. Where's a good place to begin?"

Sometimes the tutor thinks the student is making a poor decision, such as giving up too quickly on a problem and asking for the answer. The tutor might say something like this: "I'll tell you the answer if you want me to. But I think you ought to try a little longer to figure it out for yourself." But the decision is up to the student.

When there are safety problems, as in learning to drive or fly an airplane, the tutor may have to take control to avoid accidents. But otherwise, the idea is for the student to be actively in charge, with the tutor in a responsive, reactive mode.

Show Me, Let Me Try, Tell Me How I'm Doing

The basic sequence in learning, with or without a tutor, is this:

1. *Show me.* The tutor (or professor or book or film) explains and demonstrates what the student is learning to do.
2. *Let me try.* The learner begins to practice.
3. *Tell me how I'm doing.* The professor or tutor provides feedback, correcting inappropriate practice, but especially noting things done correctly or better. Practice should continue until the tutor

and the student both agree the student has mastered the material.

With this model, the tutor doesn't have to be a master teacher. He or she just has to be able to demonstrate doing the work, explain how he did it, and check the student's work.

END OF READING SPEED TEST

STOP THE TIMER

Feedback

Use this table to find your reading speed. Choose the time nearest your actual time. That will be accurate enough.

Time	Reading speed (Words per minute)
20 sec	1,521
30 sec	1,014
40 sec	760
50 sec	608
1 min	507
1 min 15 sec	405
1 min 30 sec	338
1 min 45 sec	304
2 min	253
2 min 15 sec	225
2 min 30 sec	203
2 min 45 sec	184
3 min	169
3 min 30 scc	145
4 min	127
5 min	101

Measuring Your Reading Comprehension

Now that you know your reading speed, the next step is to test your reading comprehension. In this test, do not guess. If you do not know the right answer to a question, skip it. There are no "trick" questions.

Take the five-minute reading comprehension test at:

www.PowerLearners.com/reading-level-test

Feedback

To succeed in college, it helps to read at least 300 words per minute, with 10th-grade comprehension or better. If you are not at these levels, consider working to improve. Your college probably offers some help with this. You might learn to read 400 to 500 words per minute in just a few hours. Perhaps surprisingly, as you work on speed, your comprehension also goes up.

Taking Notes

Listening to a lecture, like reading a textbook, is a way of getting ideas and information. Both can be entertaining, interesting, informative, and even exciting. Of course, both can be boring and confusing. Your mind may wander, or you may doze.

If you've faced these problems, hold on for some pleasant surprises. Surprise number one: There are notetaking techniques that can help you listen and retain information. Surprise number two: Effective notetaking does not mean writing down everything the lecturer says.

Research shows that the most successful students take fewer notes rather than more. If you try to write down everything during a lecture, you will probably miss a lot of information. You can write only about 25 words per minute, but even a slow-talking lecturer speaks at over 100 words per minute. Some speak at 150 words per minute or more. Writing out a lecture, recording it, or even taking it down in shorthand defeat the purpose of a lecture. The purpose of a lecture is to hear information presented, explained, and discussed by an expert. As you listen, you may pick up a few facts or ideas, but primarily you are after a general understanding, not a dictated textbook.

Instead of trying to write down or record a lecture, try using the following techniques to streamline both the process of taking notes and the process of studying those notes to remember the facts and understand the key ideas.

Main Ideas and Key Facts

Here is a way to take lecture notes that focuses your listening and thinking on what is important.

- Divide your notetaking paper with a vertical line. Label the left half Main Ideas. Label the right half Key Facts.
- Listen for the main ideas. Briefly note these on the left side of the paper. Expect only two or three main ideas in a one-hour lecture.
- On the right, jot down key facts, especially if you suspect they are not also in the textbook. Expect to note about ten key facts in a one-hour lecture.
- Keep your notes brief. There's no need to write a complete script of the lecture or capture all the details; that's what the textbook is for. Do note any facts about assignments and tests.
- Study your notes for a few minutes as soon as possible after class. If you didn't note a main idea, add it now. You may also want to expand or edit your notes, so they make sense when you study them later.

Example of Main Ideas/Key Facts Notes

MAIN IDEAS	KEY FACTS
Reasons behind US Revolution	Taxes, foreign troops in private homes, democracy. Some colonies had constitutions and effective self-government.
Problems	Separate colonies. No coordinated government, army or funding.
Strengths	Independent, self-reliant population. Citizens armed. Military experience from French-Indian War. History of English democracy and limited monarchy.

Practice

Use Main Ideas/Key Facts to take notes in a lecture. If you need a lecture to practice on, listen to this lecture online and take notes:

http://www.khanacademy.org/humanities/history/v/french-revolution-part-1

After the lecture, edit and, if necessary, re-write your notes to make them easier to study later.

Feedback

Compare your notes to the sample on the next page.

Sample Lecture Notes

Lecture by Salman Khan: The French Revolution (Part 1)

Main Ideas	*Key Facts*
France 1789	King Louis XVI Government and country poor After 7 years war (French & Indian War). American Revolution
	Nobility and King and Queen Marie Antoinette living it up.
	Common people going hungry, pay all the taxes, do all the work, serve and die in the army.
Enlightenment	Philosophers, scientist, some nobility and clergy think and write about democracy VS monarchy. US revolution as an example.
King calls Convocation of the Estates General	**May 1789**: Economic emergency. 1st: estate: Clergy 300 representatives, 2nd: Nobility 300, 3rd: Everybody else 600. King forced 3 estates to meet separately. 3rd estate declared themselves the National Assembly of France. King locked them out, then let them reconvene. **June**: They took the "Tennis Court Oath" to pursue their rights.
	Troops (foreign soldiers in French army) gathering in Paris. King fires adviser Neckar who was sympathetic to 3rd estate.
Storming of the Bastille	**July 14**: Citizens attack and control the Bastille. Release the 7 prisoners but get arms. Kill the commander and mayor of Paris. **August**: Declaration of the Rights of Man and of the Citizen.

Practice

Write brief answers to the following questions.

What are some advantages of taking notes using the Main Ideas/Key Facts method?

_____

_____

_____

What are possible disadvantages of this method?

_____

_____

How effective was this method compared to your usual way of taking notes?

_____

_____

More Notetaking Methods

The Main Ideas/Key Facts format is efficient and effective. But there are other notetaking methods you can consider.

Outlining

An outline is a list of main ideas, with details and supporting facts listed under each main idea. The main ideas start at the left margin of the paper; supporting facts are indented to indicate that they belong with the main idea above.

Outlining is not popular for taking notes for a very good reason. It is too much work for what you get. Trying to get everything at the right level in the outline distracts you from listening for Main Ideas and Key Facts. Also, the format implies that you are going to capture all the information in the lecture. But you don't want it all in your notes. You only want the main ideas and key facts.

After you have listened to a lecture or read a chapter in a text, creating a well-organized outline can help you organize the information you need to learn. Lecturers sometimes provide outlines of their talks, which can help you understand the material. In the end, you will learn the material by practicing. Occasionally, the best practice is to create an outline from memory.

Below is an example of a short outline prepared during a lecture or while reading, incorporating four different organizational levels.

PROFILES OF UPLAND GAME

I Pheasants
  A. Feeding
     1. Fall
     2. Winter
     3. Spring
        a. millet
  B. Nesting
  C. Habitat
II Grouse

Mind Mapping

A mind map looks somewhat like the map of a village. The main idea is the town square in the middle of the page. Less important ideas are roads leading out from the center in all directions. Small details and facts are little streets branching off the main roads. Depending on how much detail you are including, the branches may divide into smaller branches and twigs.

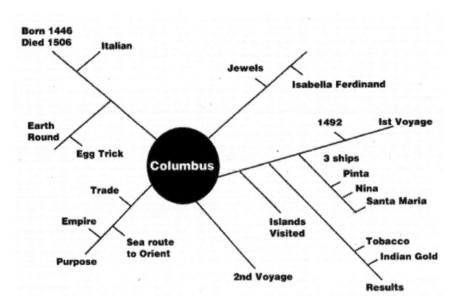

Some people like the graphic display of relationships between ideas and facts in mind maps better than lists and outlines. If you use a mind map to take lecture notes, don't try to capture all the information. The mind map you create during a lecture is likely to be a little messy. You may want to clean it up when you study.

You can create mind maps on paper or use a software app on your computer. Doing a mind map digitally makes it easier to edit and share with others. Also, it is likely to be a lot neater than one drawn by hand. A free and popular mind mapping tool is Free Mind: **http://freemind.sourceforge.net/wiki/index.php/Main_Page**

Practice

Use outlining or mind mapping to take notes in a lecture. You might even try them both. After a lecture, re-write your outline to make it more complete or better organized. If you are not currently in a lecture course, you can use this online lecture to practice these notetaking methods:

http://www.khanacademy.org/humanities/history/v/french-revolution--part-2

Which method of taking notes in a lecture do you like best? Which do you think will best help you study and master the material?

Feedback

It is your choice, of course. But we suggest that you try the Main Ideas/Key Facts approach at least a few times. It is less writing and doesn't distract you from listening and enjoying. Research supports the idea that in note taking, "less is more."

Studying from Notes

Reviewing your notes as soon as possible after a class will help you remember the information. But just reading your notes is not a strong way to practice to mastery. To understand and retain the information better, try these types of practice:

- Revise your notes. Expand and edit. Reorganize and rewrite. Go for the level of detail you need.
- Make flashcards and quiz yourself. Write key terms or questions on one side of the card. List definitions and answers on the back.

Practice

Which of the reading and notetaking methods in this lesson did you like best?

_____

_____

_____

What benefits would you get by using these methods?

_____

_____

_____

Mastery Criteria

Show your professor:

- Your reading speed and comprehension grade level.
- The flashcards you made using PRQT to study a chapter in one of your textbooks.
- The notes you took while listening to a lecture in another course or the online lecture about the French Revolution.
- Your answers to the questions above.

Lesson 6

Tests

What you'll find in this lesson are new options for preparing for tests, taking tests, and getting full value from the feedback tests provide.

Ace Tests

Preparing for Tests

How to Take Tests

After the Test: Benefit from the Feedback

Handling Stress

Ace Tests

Imagine this. You are going to take a test next week. You have a clear picture of what will be on the exam. After a little time reviewing and planning, you see that there are only a few things that you haven't mastered yet. Over the next week, you learn those things and then practice taking a practice test you create for yourself. Feeling confident and relaxed, you walk into the test without fear. There are no surprises. You work quickly but carefully, never feeling rushed or stressed. A few days later you get your test back, marked with an "A."

If this sounds like a dream, there's no need to pinch yourself. You're fully awake and firmly planted on planet Earth. The story above can happen to you. If you want to find out how, just read on.

Practice

How often have you "aced" your tests? In what subjects? In the space below, describe how you felt at those times.

_____

_____

_____

Generally, how would you rate your ability to prepare for and take tests?

_____

_____

_____

When it comes to taking tests, what skills would you like to gain or improve?

_____

_____

_____

Preparing for Tests

If you want to do well on a test, it makes sense to train—to practice on the same types of questions or problems that will be on the test. Usually, your assignments will provide that kind of practice; but not always.

Sometimes homework assignments are different from the test. For example, your professor may give you a reading assignment, but on the test, you will have to answer questions. The right way to train for this test is to practice answering questions about the information in the book.

Get the idea? To master piano playing, you practice the piano. To master solving problems in science, you solve problems. There are additional tips on taking tests in this lesson. But this one suggestion—practice doing exactly what you are learning to do—is the most powerful.

Practice

In each of the following cases, decide whether the practice matches the test. Answer Yes or No in each case.

CASE 1: Match?   YES   NO

Test: 50 short-answer questions covering the key points in chapters 1 through 4.

Practice: Answer the short-answer review questions at the end of these chapters.

CASE 2: Match?   YES   NO

Test: 50 short-answer questions covering the key points in chapters 1 through 4.

Practice: Read the chapters carefully, trying to remember the key points.

CASE 3: Match?   YES   NO

Test: Five essay questions in which you support your opinions about current events with facts from history.

Practice: Read the chapters carefully, trying to remember the key points.

CASE 4: Match?   YES   NO

Test: Five essay questions in which you support your opinions with facts from history.

Practice: Answer the short-answer review questions at the end of each chapter.

Feedback

CASE 1:

Test: 50 short-answer questions covering the key points in chapters 1 through 4.

Practice: Answer the short-answer review questions at the end of each chapter.

Match? **Yes**, the practice matches the test. This is especially so if the review questions are similar in form and content to those the professor includes on the test.

CASE 2:

Test: 50 short-answer questions covering the key points in chapters 1 through 4.

Practice: Read the chapters carefully, trying to remember the key points.

Match? **No**. The practice indicated does not involve answering questions. It may help, but it is not sufficient.

CASE 3:

Test: Five essay questions in which you support your opinions about current events with facts from history.

Practice: Read the chapters carefully, trying to remember the key points.

Match? **No**. Only answering essay questions will prepare you for this test.

CASE 4:

Test: Five essay questions in which you support your opinions with facts from history.

Practice: Answer the short-answer review questions at the end of each chapter.

Match? **No**. The practice described does not prepare you for answering essay questions. Note that the right practice for this test is to sit down and write your opinions about a topic, supported by facts from history. No kidding. Think about a football scrimmage. The team practices for a game by running plays. You practice for this history course by answering essay questions. Yyou should do this enough so that you can answer five essay questions in one hour, just as you will have to do on the test.

Additional Tips on Taking Tests

Master Every Assignment

Mastering each assignment in a course, starting from day one, puts you on solid ground for taking tests. If you haven't done this, you might still have time to practice to mastery on some of the material—maybe all of it.

Remember that mastering material now helps you to retain that material longer and to learn additional material faster. The extra time you spend mastering every assignment can reduce the total hours needed to get the grade you want. As you master each assignment, you will find that your confidence and motivation grow.

Create Your Own Study Aids

Make flashcards, outlines, or mind maps. Just creating these aids can help. Create these aids as you go along so you will have them for both the current exam and the final. In a course that involves labeling diagrams, or timelines, make copies before you fill them in. That way, you'll have blanks to use for practice when you study for exams. Depending on your course, you might make three copies: use one to prepare for the next quiz or exam, one for the midterm exam, and the third for the final exam.

Drill and Review Often

Move information from short-term memory to long-term memory by reviewing and studying several times over a period of days or weeks.

Find out the Ground Rules

Professors will tell you what materials you can use during the test. They may also explain how they grade. For example, they may impose a guessing penalty for wrong answers. On essay questions, some professors may subtract points for spelling and grammar; others may only grade on the content and organization of your writing.

Many professors will tell you what type of questions to expect, and how many questions of each type will be on the exam.

Find Out What Will Be on the Test

During class and office hours, many professors will provide information about what to study for their exams.

If you don't know some vital information about a test, the professor may not have provided it, or you may have missed it. Either way, don't stay in the dark. For openers, you can ask your professor. Depending upon the professor, you might ask, "What will be on the test?" To avoid sounding like you are asking for an unfair advantage, you might better ask, "What type of questions will be on the test? How many questions will there be? Can you suggest what information or chapters to focus on? How do you suggest I study?"

Even with all the information the professor has been willing to reveal, you may not have sufficient information about a test to prepare effectively. In that case, here are some more suggestions.

Get Old Tests

Save your exams in each course. Usually, a professor's exams are similar throughout the course. Another good reference would be old exams you might get from someone who took the course last year.

Some professors use the same exams over and over. If so, they will generally collect all old exams. Maybe you can get advice from people who had this professor last year. Their experiences and memories may be a great help to you.

Meet with Your Professor

Many professors have conference or office hours scheduled for meeting with students. And often the hours pass without a taker. That time could be yours for the asking.

Some people fear that professors use meetings to find out what students don't know and lower their grades. On the contrary, most professors are impressed by students who make the extra effort to show up. Go ahead. Knock on that door. You may find your professor even more helpful during office hours than in class.

Make an Educated Guess

No matter how many or how few of the above suggestions you follow, you usually cannot be certain what will be on the test. So, when the time comes to prepare, you may have to make an educated guess—your best estimate of what will be covered and with what types of questions or problems. To do that, here are two suggestions.

First, make a list of what you are expected to know. The amount of material in a course can seem overwhelming, even when it isn't. So, your topic list may be surprisingly short. Even if the list is long, you're better off facing it than ignoring it.

Second, create your own practice test. Based on everything you know about the coming test, the course, and the professor, make up your own test. You can use questions from class, the textbook, handouts, and assignments. If you can't find any questions on some material, write your own. Make up the kinds of questions your professor would ask, aiming for a realistic number of questions.

Test Yourself

Sports teams practice by scrimmaging. In other words, to prepare for a game, they play practice games. The same idea can work for you: Use your practice test as a scrimmage. Actually test yourself with a time limit.

If you know the material well, you first test yourself and then brush up on the few things you need to improve.

On the other hand, if you are not up to date in a course, study first. Practice reciting, answering or solving questions and problems like those on your practice test. Plan how you will learn each topic and estimate the time that will take. Make a schedule to do that learning and keep to it. Once you have brought yourself up to speed, then take the practice test to spot any weak areas you'll want to strengthen further.

In some courses with some professors, you may find the tests difficult because of the types of questions. Many students find essay questions scary, for example. In cases like that, it makes sense for you to practice answering essay questions several times. You may have to make up several practice tests to get enough practice.

Practice

Suppose your Literature professor provides this information about the midterm exam: There will be three essay questions on Shakespeare's *Macbeth*. One question will be worth 50 points; each of the other two will be worth 25 points. The test will be 50 minutes. No books or notes allowed.

The questions will be on the topics we are discussing in class. The questions will be like, but not necessarily the same as, these examples:

1. Why did Macbeth murder the king?
2. Describe the personality of Lady Macbeth.
3. What did Shakespeare have to say about friendship?

Use a worksheet in the LearningPlan spreadsheet to describe how you would prepare for this exam.

Feedback

Your plan should certainly include creating a practice test of 3 essay questions and taking the test with a 50-minute time limit. No kidding! This is how to ensure that you do well on tests.

In preparing for the test, you would take the practice test and then analyze your performance. You would consider whether your answers were both accurate and well written. If you are uncertain about how well you did, you could get feedback from your professor or a classmate or two. If you didn't do as well as you want, change the questions on your practice exam and test yourself again.

Practice

For one of your other courses, create a practice test you could use to prepare for the next quiz or exam. After creating the test, how would you prepare to take the test? Do that preparation. Then test yourself.

_____

_____

_____

_____

How would you compare this approach to how you prepared for tests in the past?

_____

_____

_____

_____

How to Take Tests

Come fully equipped

Make a list of the things you want to have on hand during the test. If allowed, bring your textbook. Other common items include a dictionary, calculator, pencils, and erasers. To avoid added stress the morning of the test, gather these things the night before.

Warm up before the test

On the morning of the test, spend a few minutes going over the material you've studied. Here the purpose is not to learn anything new but to warm up a few brain circuits and get your mind in gear. So, make a quick mind map or outline. If you have some flashcards, do a short drill. For a math or science test, solve a problem or two.

Arrive early

If you arrive late, you lose time for answering questions. Arriving early gives you time to get settled and even use some of the relaxation techniques described later in this lesson.

Read the directions

Some bank executives in Minneapolis wanted to see if anyone was reading the literature the bank was mailing to customers. So, in one of their brochures, the bank included a sentence that offered $50 to anyone who simply wrote and asked for it. They had no takers.

There probably won't be any cash offers in the test directions you read. But there may be tips that earn you points. Test directions don't exist merely to take up space on paper. Read them carefully, and you may find information that can make a real difference in your grade. For example, you might find that the directions tell you to answer any three of four questions.

Budget your time

Test taking is like treasure hunting. The goal is to gather up as many of the goods—in this case, points—as you can. To walk away with some real gold, set priorities. A question's worth is measured in points. So, the aim is to look at the point value of each question and give it the time and energy it's worth—no less, no more.

Take a moment at the beginning of a test to notice how many points the various questions are worth. Budget your time per question. If all the questions have the same value, divide your time equally. Don't spend more time on a question than it is worth.

If the questions have different values, allocate your time based on points. If there are 100 total points and you have 50 minutes, that is an average of 2 points per minute. For a 10-point question, budget 5 minutes; for a 20-point question, allow 10 minutes.

Review your work

Even if you haven't finished all the questions, take a few minutes at the end to check your work. Make sure your name is on each piece of paper, and that the pages and answers are numbered. Look over your work and make any last-minute corrections. You might be surprised at the answers that cry out for fixing.

After the Test: Benefit from the Feedback

When the exam is over, it is not unusual to feel some upset or to avoid thinking about it. That's natural. But, there may be some value in taking a few minutes to focus on anything you did or didn't do that worked well. Switch your focus from what went wrong to what went right. This will help you do more of the right stuff next time.

Calm down before you do this. If you are still cursing yourself or the professor or the test, you are not yet ready.

When you are calm and focused, think about specifics. Compare the actual test to your practice test. Were your educated guesses correct? Did you study the right material? Were the questions of the same type as you used for practice? If so, take a bow.

Did you do the right kinds of practice? With what questions and topics did practicing to mastery help on the test? If any of this was true, congratulations. You are becoming a Power Learner.

This is how it works. Figure out what you need or want to be able to do. Practice doing it, getting any help you need. Persevere to mastery. DO GREAT ON TESTS.

Handling Stress

Throughout our years in school, some of us learn one thing perfectly: How to fear tests. If you have test anxiety, here are some techniques that can make a huge difference.

These methods are based on visualizing our fears. In other words, to overcome a fear, confront it intentionally. See it, deal with it, and then put it aside.

Visualize the night before

Use this process the night before a test, or anytime you're worrying about an upcoming test or assignment.

1. Confront the worst possibility. Imagine that what you fear is taking place. Feel the fear, failure, humiliation, and embarrassment. Make the scene as real as you can. For example:

   I see myself going into class and reading through the questions. I sit there feeling as dumb as a pillow because I don't understand any of them. My heart is racing, and I get that knot in the pit of my stomach. My hand is shaking too much for me to hold a pencil. I start to feel dizzy, and the room starts spinning. Pretty soon everything is dark. I'm passed out on the floor, and I can't get up. Everyone is laughing. They think I've faked it. This is my last chance to pass the course, and I've truly blown it...

Having looked in detail at failing, notice that you will probably survive.

2. Fear, like all feelings, consists of thoughts and body sensations. To reduce your fears, focus on both. Go back through the scene and feel the fear in your body. Identify the physical symptoms of the fear: that tension in the stomach, the sweaty hands or lump in your throat. Then, with your mind's eye, study each sensation. As you focus on it, the sensations usually start to fade. Go back and forth between picturing the worst possible situation and noticing sensations in your body. Keep doing this until most of the emotional charge or upset dissipates.

3. Let that worst possible outcome drift off. You've already done it in your mind. It's out of the way, so now you can let it go.

4. Finally, create a vivid picture of success. Imagine yourself breezing through the test, at ease and relaxed. You know the answers; you feel good about yourself. Already you know how good it will feel to get the test back with the grade you want. Picture that grade written in red on the front of your test paper.

Sometimes this technique of visualizing what we fear works great. Try it. It takes only a few minutes and might make you feel better and do better.

Practice

Imagine that tomorrow you will have an exam in some specific course. For this exercise, think about a course that was or is difficult for you. For that course and exam, practice the "night before" visualization procedure described above.

Feedback

Did this technique work for you? Might you try it in the future?

Visualize right before the test

Just before a test, or even during the test, you can return to the positive picture you created (step 4, above). Hold that positive vision in your mind for a few moments. In your mind, zoom in on that scene and make it as bright and colorful as you can. Then go to work on the test.

Practice

Imagine that it is the day of the test—the same test you just used for the "night before" visualization. Do the "before the test" visualization.

Feedback

Did this technique work for you? Might you try it in the future?

Mastery Criteria

Go through the suggestions in this lesson about preparing for and taking tests. Put a check mark next to those that you already do. Put a star or asterisk next to those that you intend to start using.

Discuss your test-taking approaches, past difficulties and the new methods in this lesson with your professor.

Lesson 7

Setting Goals and Reaching Them

This lesson will guide you in rethinking your goals. Then you will learn the Change Process, which is a useful way to change old habits and develop better ones.

Setting Long-term, Intermediate, and Short-Term Goals

The Change Process

Setting Goals

Dreams are pleasant. But to get what you dream of, convert those dreams into goals and commit to actions to achieve them. For this, it helps to set long-term, intermediate, and short-term goals.

Set long-term goals

Most of us have some notion of what we want in life—things like being happy, making enough money, having a family, or being a professional athlete. These wonderful thoughts are the starting point for defining your own specific goals. The more specific your goals, the more likely you are to achieve them.

The first step in goal setting is to set your long-term and life goals. These are goals that will probably take more than one year to achieve. They may take five years or even 25 years. Following are examples of long-term goals:

- Graduate from college by age 22
- Travel around the world by age 30
- Get married and have children
- Have a career as a professional baseball player
- Become a millionaire
- Help people
- Earn my living as an actress
- Become a doctor
- Learn to sail
- Own a Ferrari
- End hunger in the world

When setting goals, there are no right or wrong answers. You may not have decided on your career or having a family. That's O.K.

As you learn more about yourself and have more experience, expect your long-term goals to change.

Practice

Spend five minutes brainstorming your own long-term goals. This means letting your mind roam. In the space below, jot down long-term goals as they occur to you, so you don't forget. Don't evaluate or analyze while brainstorming. If something comes to mind, write it down.

_____

_____

_____

_____

_____

_____

After brainstorming, spend five minutes looking over your list. Think about what you wrote and additions and changes.

Finally, select the three long-term goals that are most important to you. If you have a computer or laptop, type those three goals. Otherwise, write them here.

_____

_____

_____

Feedback

As you continue through this lesson, you may decide to change one or more of your goals. If so, go ahead and make the change.

Set intermediate goals

To reach your long-term goals and enjoy a satisfying life along the way, it helps to define intermediate goals. These are things you can accomplish in one year or less. Here are some examples of intermediate goals:

- Learn three new dance steps this semester
- Buy a used car by summer
- Earn a 3.5 grade average this semester
- Get an A in Spanish
- Consistently make 50 percent of my free throws in basketball
- Manage my time so that I routinely turn in assignments when they are due

Practice

With your long-term goals in mind, spend five minutes brainstorming all the things you would like to accomplish this year. Include any outcomes leading toward your long-term goals, as well as activities you'll find satisfying and enjoyable this year.

_____

_____

_____

_____

Now spend another five minutes reviewing your intermediate goals. Make any additions or corrections that you wish. Finally, select six or fewer intermediate goals for this year, type them up and print them out. Or, if you are not using a word proccssor, write them here.

_____   _____

_____   _____

_____   _____

Feedback

If you have any questions about your long-term and intermediate goals, ask your professor.

Set short-term goals

To advance toward your long-term and intermediate goals, you are likely to find it useful to set some weekly and monthly goals. You can then use your To-Do List and calendar to manage your activities from day to day.

Here are some examples of short-term goals.

- Do all my chores
- Complete all assignments for this week
- Work six hours and put $50 in the bank
- Arrange a bowling party for Saturday night

Practice

In the next five minutes brainstorm short-term goals for this week and month that will move you in the direction of your intermediate and long-term goals.

_____

_____

_____

_____

_____

Type up your short-term goals. Or, write them here.

_____

_____

_____

_____

_____

Print or write your long-term, intermediate and short-term goals on a sheet of paper. We suggest pinning them up some place you look often, such as above your desk. Referring to your goals often and keeping them in mind will help you focus on doing the tasks that move you toward them.

Feedback

You have just spent about half an hour setting your goals. Perhaps you noticed some benefits from this exercise right away—such as feeling more in-charge or excited to get started.

The Change Process

Most of us can list areas in our lives where things aren't working as well as we would like. Often there are many things we would like to change. We may want to reduce or eliminate problems. Or we may want to improve how we do things and our results. We may want to change our own habits, make new ones, or change what other people do.

The Change Process can help. There are seven steps, described below. The Change Process doesn't fit every situation, and it won't always work. But many people have found it helpful and you may, too.

There are two key ideas behind the Change Process. First, we humans can change what we do and how we do it. In other words, we are not necessarily stuck with how we are now. This opens lots of possibilities. Of course, changing your regular habits or ways of doing things can be difficult and maybe embarrassing. Still, it can be done.

Second, it is difficult to change someone else. You may have tried polite requests, persuasion, or even threats. Still, you may have had little success. Well, in the Change Process, you are asked to consider a different approach. To get someone else to change, change yourself. This may seem like giving in or selling out. It may seem unfair that you must change rather than the other person. But if what you have been doing in the past hasn't worked, why not try something new? So, part of the Change Process is to look for useful ways to change what you control, namely yourself.

Here are the steps in the Change Process. Read these through. Then there's a practice to try it. Perhaps your professor will lead you through the process the first time.

Step 1: Goal

Begin by saying what you want to change. For example, you might say, "I want to get a least a B in math." Or maybe, "I'd like my parents to stop nagging me about choosing a major." It might be something you want to change about yourself, like getting more sleep or not procrastinating so much. Whatever it is, say it to yourself and write it down, so you're clear about the change you want.

Step 2: Responsibility

Take responsibility for the current situation. It may be that you don't feel responsible. You may blame someone else for the situation—a parent, professor or friend, for example. Still, think about what you are doing or not doing that might be contributing to the problem.

The reason to do this is that you can more easily change yourself than other people. So, finding any way you contribute to the problem may help you find a better or easier way to fix it. For example, suppose your issue is your roommates nagging you to keep the apartment clean. You might notice how clean or messy it is and your role in causing some of the mess. For the moment, don't worry about fixing the situation; just accept responsibility for anything you do or don't do that contributes to it.

Step 3: Forgiveness

Forgive yourself for the way things have been up to now. Be understanding of yourself, even if you caused some or all the problems. The Perfect Human Being Society is a club with no members.

Step 4: Brainstorm

Brainstorming is a quick way to come up with ideas. Allow 5 to 10 minutes and come up with as many different solutions to your issue as you can. Don't worry about whether an idea is good or workable. Jot it down and try to think of more new ideas.

For example, to handle an issue with your roommates about cleaning, noise, privacy or expenses.

- Convince roommates to respect the privacy of my room.
- Keep the door closed.
- Hire a maid to clean the apartment.
- Clean up every morning before going out.
- Buy a cabinet for storage.
- Buy a laundry hamper for dirty clothes.
- Get my compulsive roommate to see a psychologist about cleanliness.
- Move out.

Step 5: Action Plan

Stop brainstorming and figure out which of your ideas might be practical. Then decide on a plan of action. Write the one or more things you intend to do in the next week to improve the situation. It doesn't have to be something big. Sometimes a little change can have a big impact.

Step 6: Practice

Implement your action plan as best you can. As you practice, you will master it. If the plan is working, that will help motivate you to continue. If you slip into your old behaviors, that's natural. Notice it, forgive yourself, and then continue practicing the new behavior.

Step 7: Feedback

In about a week, think about whether what you are doing is working and getting you closer to your goal. If so, keep practicing. If not, go to Step 1 and cycle through the process again.

Practice

A good way to learn the Change Process is to ask your professor to guide you through the process as you try to change something in your life to get the results you want.

The steps are:

- Goal
- Responsibility
- Forgiveness
- Brainstorm
- Action Plan
- Practice
- Feedback

Mastery Criteria

- Discuss the goal-setting process and your long-term, intermediate and short-term goals with your professor.
- Use the Change Process to change what you are doing that could eliminate a problem or improve results.

Lesson 8

The Writing Process

In this lesson you will master a writing process—specific steps to overcome procrastination, choose your topic, organize information, and quickly produce a first draft of any writing assignment. In the next lesson, you'll learn about revising and editing that first draft to produce polished prose that will engage your audience and earn you high grades.

Try a New Writing Process

Make Friends with Both Sides of Your Brain

A 5-Step Writing Process

4 Quick Ways to Get Organized

Organize by Clustering Keywords

Try a New Writing Process

This lesson is about handling any writing assignment more effectively and quickly; maybe even with pleasure. The assignment might be a term paper or the answer to an essay question. It might be an essay you write to apply to another college or a cover letter to apply for a job. Whatever your assignment, the process you learn in this lesson will enable you to write better, in less time.

Maybe the first thought that occurs to you is, "Writing, yuk! Maybe there's a way I can skip this lesson!" That thought is understandable, especially if you've had trouble with writing in the past.

Consider the choice you have right here, right now. You could decide to go through the motions and get through this lesson without really working at it. If you do, your writing and your feelings about writing are likely to stay the same as they are now. But if you commit to practicing a new approach, you could totally change your experience of writing.

This lesson presents a complete writing process that has helped thousands of students improve their writing. It will take you about 3 hours or less to master this process. Invest those three hours and you could save much more than that on your very next writing assignment.

Practice

How do you feel about writing?

_____

_____

_____

_____

_____

_____

What things would you like to change about your writing and about doing writing assignments?

_____

_____

_____

_____

_____

_____

_____

_____

_____

_____

_____

Make Friends with Both Sides of Your Brain

As you probably know, the left and right sides of your brain do different kinds of tasks. In our writing process, some of the steps are analytical, "left-brain" tasks. Others are creative, "right-brain" tasks. Both types of thinking are necessary—but not at the same time. In learning the process, you may find it helpful to know which part of the brain is best for each step.

Here are some differences between the two sides of the brain.

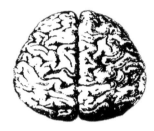

https://creativecommons.org/licenses/by-sa/3.0/

LEFT BRAIN	RIGHT BRAIN
Controls right arm and leg	Controls left arm and leg
Controls speech	Controls rhythmic activity such as dance and playing musical instruments
Notices details	Looks at the whole
Thinks logically	Responds to images
Processes facts and rules	Notices emotions and feelings

In the writing process, you first plan what you are going to write about and your purpose. That's a "left-brain" logical task. Then you can use brainstorming, which is a "right-brain," creative task. The table below shows the steps of the writing process steps and which side of your brain is used to do them. As you can see, the process moves from a left-brain task to a right-brain task, and back again. Knowing this should help you keep the steps straight and to do them better.

The Writing Process

LEFT BRAIN (Analytical)	RIGHT BRAIN (Creative)
Plan	
	Brainstorm Ideas and Facts
Organize Before Writing a Draft	
	Write First Draft
Revise and Edit	

These steps are described below. After reading through them, you will learn them by practicing.

A 5-Step Writing Process

Here is a summary of the steps in this writing process. Read through the steps as a preview, then there are directions and exercises you'll use to practice and master the steps.

1 **Plan**—Start with the big picture. Choose your audience, purpose, and subject. Also, understand the specific requirements for your assignment.

2 **Brainstorm**—Take a few minutes to think: daydream, doodle, draw, or even stare into space for a little while. Perhaps this will seem like procrastinating. Actually, it is a good way to sift through ideas, noting those that you can use in your writing. Then, take a few more minutes to jot down Keywords for any ideas, facts, and topics that you might include in what you are writing.

3 **Organize**—After you jot down those Keywords, use your analytical left-brain to organize. Do this by writing Key Sentences or Clustering Keywords. Organizing before drafting saves a lot of re-organizing and re-writing later.

4 **Draft**—This is what people usually think of as writing. Using your creative, right-brain abilities, write your first draft quickly, without regard for grammar, punctuation, or getting the words "right." Don't expect to produce polished writing for your first draft.

5 **Edit**—Now you change from writer to editor. This is a big deal. In Lesson 9 you will learn a great way to do this. By consciously separating drafting from editing, you will dramatically improve the design and content of your draft. Then edit and polish your draft for clear, grammatical and impactful communication.

Working through this lesson, you will practice and master steps one through four. In the next lesson, you will practice editing.

Practice

Next to each step in the table below, indicate whether it is a left-brain or right-brain task. Then enter the letter of the best description of the task from this list.

A. The first writing of the composition, done quickly without concern for grammar, punctuation, or correct wording.
B. Defining the audience and your purpose for writing.
C. Defining the order in which the material is presented to the reader.
D. Polishing the writing so it communicates clearly.
E. Jotting down Keywords for ideas, facts and topics that come to mind.

Step	Left (Analytical)	Right (Creative)	Description
PLAN			
BRAINSTORM			
ORGANIZE			
DRAFT			
EDIT			

Feedback

Next to each step in the table below, indicate whether it is a left-brain or right-brain task. Then enter the letter of the best description of the task from this list.

A. The first writing of the composition, done quickly without concern for grammar, punctuation, or correct wording.
B. Defining the audience and your purpose for writing.
C. Defining the order in which the material is presented to the reader.
D. Polishing the writing so it communicates clearly.
E. Jotting down Keywords for ideas, facts and topics that come to mind.

Step	Left (Analytical)	Right (Creative)	Description
PLAN	X		B
BRAINSTORM		X	E
ORGANIZE	X		C
DRAFT		X	A
EDIT	X		D

If you are uncertain of your answers about the steps in the writing process, ask your professor or another student to check your work.

Detailed Descriptions of the 5 Steps

Step 1: Getting a Jump Start with Planning

Great papers start with a plan, the first step in our writing process. In planning an essay, you specify:

- Audience
- Purpose
- Topic
- Specific requirements

The plan for many school essays could be something like this:

- *Audience:* Your professor.
- *Purpose:* To complete the assignment.
- *Topic:* Assigned topic, sometimes my choice from a list.
- Specific requirements: 1,500 words.

This plan makes sense because your professor may be the only person who reads your essay. And perhaps your primary purpose is to meet the requirements and get a good grade.

But, if you want to learn something new about writing, then consider a different approach. Choose an audience other than your professor and a purpose other than just getting the assignment completed. Doing so opens more options. First, you are more likely to learn about the subject, which may be the primary reason your professor gave you this assignment. Second, you will practice learning by gathering facts, analyzing those facts, and coming to conclusions you and others can use. In other words, you will be practicing one of the primary tools we use to understand and solve problems in academics, business and life. Finally, this will undoubtedly be more fun and get you a better grade.

Here's an example. Suppose there's an artist who is a master at painting sunsets. She makes her living by painting pictures and selling them. So, you might say the artist's audience is some person who will buy the painting, and the artist's purpose is to make pictures that sell. That's one possible way to plan her work.

There are other options as well. The artist might say to herself, "Looking at the ocean today, I feel happy. I will choose this purpose: I want most people who look at this painting to feel happy." At other times, her purpose might be to capture the beauty of the sunset or to portray the vastness of the sea and sky. Any of these purposes could guide her in the actual painting.

You may have heard that true art is never done only to make money; that a real artist is motivated by a desire to create. Perhaps that is true. But it is also true that many artists and writers intend to sell their work. So, they have two purposes—to create and to sell.

When it comes to writing, you can have two purposes as well. Your first purpose may be to get "paid" with a good grade. But you can select a second purpose to guide you in creating a great essay. Some possible purposes might be:

- Inform readers.
- Interest readers in something new.
- Change your readers' minds about an issue.
- Persuade readers to take some action.
- Amuse or entertain your readers.
- Tell a story that moves the reader.

Here are some school examples. Imagine that you're writing a lab report for biology. Your purpose might be to inform readers about your observations. In other cases, your purpose might be to convince lawmakers to increase taxes so that there is more money for schools. Your purpose in writing a book report might be to inform readers about the main ideas in the book. And your secondary purposes for the book report might be to amuse your readers and convince them to read the book.

In school, a plan might be something like this:

Audience—interested and educated people who do not know the subject as well as you do, or who have reached conclusions different from yours.

Purpose—to inform the reader about a topic, or to change the reader's view on some subject. Meeting this purpose often means including facts and information, and then drawing your conclusions or making recommendations to the reader. In writing short stories, poems, or letters, you can choose a more emotional or personal purpose—for example, to convey emotion or humor.

Topic—the assigned topic or a topic of your choice, depending upon the assignment. Even when your professor chooses the topic, write as though you had chosen it yourself.

Specific requirements—Specific requirements are not just part of school assignments. Technical writers, advertising copywriters, and other professional writers almost always work to a specified number of words. Even novelists generally write books in the range from 300 to 600 pages.

Practice

Suppose your English literature professor has just given you an essay assignment. You are required to write an essay on *Moby Dick*, the book you have just finished reading for that class. You are asked to describe and analyze the personality of Captain Ahab. Your essay cannot be longer than five pages.

Create a plan for this essay by choosing items from the list below.

1. Your audience is
   _____

2. Your purpose is
   _____

3. Your topic is
   _____

4. The specific
   requirements are
   _____

a.	A summary of a whaling adventure story.	j	To discuss the psychological motivations behind Captain Ahab's actions.
b.	Captain Ahab's personality.		
c.	To write about a whale.	k.	To get a good grade.
d.	To describe the actions of Captain Ahab.	1.	To spend as little time as possible.
e.	Five pages.	m.	To amuse the professor.
f.	Five pages or less.	n.	To amuse the reader.
g.	A person interested in literature.	o.	To convince someone to read Moby Dick.
h.	Your professor.	p.	Other people who have read Moby Dick.
i.	Your classmates.		

Feedback

1. g
2. d and j, and maybe, also, k, l, m, n, and o.
3. b
4. f

Step 2: Brainstorming

Once you have done your planning, brainstorming is a powerful way to overcome procrastination and gather your thoughts about what you want to say.

Here's how to brainstorm:

- At the top of a blank sheet of paper, write the topic of your essay.

- Relax. Get comfortable. Close your eyes or look out the window. Take a few deep breaths and let the tension in your muscles melt away. When you are breathing a little more deeply, begin the next step.

- Create an image in your mind that relates to your topic. Then write down a word or phrase that describes the image. As the next thought or image comes to mind, write words that describe it. Continue jotting down these Keywords, naming people, places, things, and ideas you might include in your essay.

Brainstorming is a "right-brain" activity. It works best if you just let your mind roam and write down whatever comes to you. Try not to evaluate or analyze your thoughts. If an idea or picture comes to your mind, jot down a Keyword and move on. Later, after brainstorming, you can scratch out words that don't fit.

Brainstorming might take two to five minutes—enough time to list 10 to 20 items. And it sure beats staring at a blank page, trying to start the first sentence.

A list of Keywords brainstormed for an essay on the topic of My Summer Vacation might look like this:

England	restaurant
London	jogging
Hanover Hotel	Laundromat
rental car	airplane
Tower of London	Brighton
Harrods Dept. Store	luggage
Hard Rock Cafe	

Practice

For this exercise in brainstorming, suppose you get an assignment to write a letter to a friend about anything that has happened to you recently. Here's how to use brainstorming to get started.

- Write the topic you will brainstorm about in the space provided below.
  TOPIC: _____

- Relax for a minute or two. Sit in a comfortable position. Gaze out the window or at the room and daydream a little.

- Brainstorm. When you feel relaxed, begin to look at recent events in your life. Think about any major events or experiences that you liked or disliked. Jot down a word or two to describe the thoughts and images that come to mind.

Don't censor yourself. As each thought or picture comes to mind, write down a Keyword or two to describe it. Continue brainstorming until you have at least 10 Keywords. If that takes you longer than five minutes, ask your professor for advice on brainstorming.

Since this is an exercise in brainstorming, don't write the letter. Just make your list of Keywords.

KEYWORDS:

_____

_____

_____

Step 3: Organize Before Writing a Draft

The next step is to organize your paper. Here's what many professional writers do. Based on their Keywords, they write 5 to 10 Key Sentences. These sentences fill in more detail about the Keywords, but this is not the first draft of your paper. It is a short list of sentences covering the key ideas for your essay.

Organizing with Key Sentences is a left-brain process. You are thinking about what you will say and what you will not. You may use sentences which don't include any of your Keywords. You can also ignore Keywords which now seem irrelevant. With a little practice, writing your Key Sentences can take just 15 minutes or less. When you've captured the idea in a single Key Sentence, move on to the next idea. Write your Key Sentences quickly. They can be in any order. Don't worry about spelling, punctuation, or grammar. Even incomplete sentences and phrases are OK for now.

Keep generating Key Sentences until you've covered the points and ideas suggested by your Keywords. Depending upon the length of the composition, that might be five to 15 sentences. You may find it helpful to check off each Keyword as you use it in a Key Sentence. Also, cross out Keywords for any ideas or facts that you decide to leave out.

Following are Key Sentences to go with the Keywords about My Summer Vacation. Note that the sentences are not in any special order.

Last summer I was able to take a trip to London.

Getting ready to go was frantic and I got even more excited on the plane.

At the Hard Rock Café we met a great bunch of kids who were headed for Brighton for the weekend.

We saw the usual tourist spots—Tower of London.

We found a reasonable room at the Hanover.

I liked the clothes at Harrods but English food was unappealing and expensive.

I jogged most mornings, tennis at Battersea Park.

On the way home, I could barely fit my new clothes in my suitcase and backpack.

Practice

Write Key Sentences for your letter to a friend in the space provided below. Refer to the Keywords you brainstormed in the last Practice. (Note: Do not write the letter. Key Sentences may be short, almost like a topic or heading. They are not a draft.)

_____

_____

_____

_____

_____

_____

_____

_____

_____

_____

_____

Step 3 (Continued): Sequencing Key Sentences

To further organize your writing, you decide what idea comes first, what comes second, and so on. If you are working with paper and pencil, you don't have to rewrite the Key Sentences; just put a number next to each one to indicate the order. With word processing, it is easy and maybe more convenient to rearrange the sentences in the order you want.

When you are done numbering or rearranging, read the Key Sentences in order and decide whether this arrangement makes sense. If not, change the order. It may take several tries before you say to yourself, "Aha! That's it. Here is an arrangement that works."

Numbering the Key Sentences in logical order saves time later. That's because rearranging an essay can take a lot of rewriting. Resequencing Key Sentences is quick and easy.

Practice

Here is another list of Key Sentences. Number the sentences in the order you would write about them in an essay. After numbering them, read the sentences in numbered order to another classmate. Does the order make sense to both of you? If not, renumber the sentences and read them again. Continue until the order makes sense.

Topic: Choosing UCLA

	UCLA is near Hollywood.
	My aunt and uncle live in LA.
	I'm planning to go to UCLA in the fall.
	To go to college out of state was too expensive.
	I'd like to study pre-law or computers.
	I wanted to be away from home, but close to some of my family.
	I don't mind a large university.
	I like the buildings at UCLA especially the library.

Feedback

There is not just one right answer. Here is one possibility:

6 UCLA is near Hollywood.

8 My aunt and uncle live in LA.

1 I'm planning to go to UCLA in the fall.

3 To go to college out of state was too expensive.

2 I'd like to study pre-law or computers.

7 I wanted to be away from home, but close to some of my family.

4 I don't mind a large university.

5 I like the buildings at UCLA, especially the library.

If you had difficulty doing this practice, consult your professor.

Four Quick Ways to Get Organized

There are some common ways to organize essays and reports. No one way is right for every situation, and there are many variations on these basic approaches. Still, these four are very useful.

1. Time Sequence

Describe events in the order in which they occurred. Novels, plays, short stories, history books, mysteries, letters about your vacation trip—all these are examples where organizing by time sequence could be a good choice.

2. Location or Position

Describe things based on their location, or the order in which you encounter them. For a book report, for example, you might discuss the chapters in order. A geography text might describe the countries of Europe moving from the northwest down to the southeast. An astronomy paper could discuss the planets in order of their distance from the sun.

3. Describe, Analyze, Recommend (or Conclude)

Essays, book reports, business letters, and technical reports often use this approach. Here the author starts by stating an issue or posing a problem to solve. Then the author analyzes the issue, discussing the facts and ideas involved. Finally, the author recommends some course of action or draws some conclusion. Sometimes the recommendations or conclusions are summarized at the beginning. For example: "Today 8,000 children around the world will die of malnutrition. There are four things you can do about it."

4. Overview, Major Facts, Minor Facts

Many authors want to communicate many facts and ideas on a topic. In this case, they may arrange those items in the order of their importance. Newspaper articles often use this approach.

Practice

For each of the following situations, choose an organizing concept which you consider appropriate. There aren't any wrong answers, so choose an approach you would use. The choices are:

- Time Sequence
- Location or Position
- Describe, Analyze, Recommend (or Conclude)
- Overview, Major Facts, Minor Facts

1. Write to a friend about your walking around an interesting city while on vacation.

_____

2. Describe to a friend, why you are considering buying a particular make and model of car.

_____

3. Write your autobiography.

_____

4. Write an essay on how you think students should choose their representatives to student government.

_____

Feedback

Some workable choices are these:

1. Write to a friend describing a walk you took while on vacation in an interesting city.
    Organize by Location

2. Describe your new car to a friend, indicating why you chose that make and model.
    Organize by Overview, Major facts, Minor facts

3. Write your autobiography.
    Organize by Time Sequence

4. Write an essay on how you think students should choose their representatives to student government.
    Organize by Describe, Analyze, Recommend

Organize by Clustering Keywords

So far in this lesson, you've learned how to brainstorm and jot down Keywords, create Key Sentences, and number the sentences in sequence. Many students and professional writers use and love this approach just as it is. Others use Clustering of Keywords rather than Key Sentences. Here's how Clustering works.

Suppose you want to write an essay on the airlines. Your list of Keywords could include:

airlines	flight attendant service
expansion plans	waiting lines
airline food	airport parking
late departures	small seats
noisy planes	too many planes
regional airports	buses to airport

Instead of writing Key Sentences, cluster the Keywords around topics, like this:

waiting line	
airport parking	
noisy planes	Topic: airport problems
too many planes	

expansion plans	
regional airports	Topic: solutions
buses to airport	

airline food	
late departures	Topic: in-flight problems
small seats	

Each cluster of words could form one section of the essay. Number the clusters in a logical order, and Presto— you are organized.

Practice

Number the Clusters above in a logical order.

Feedback

There is no one correct order. One possibility would be:

waiting line	
airport parking	
noisy planes	Topic: airport problems **1.**
too many planes	

expansion plans	
regional airports	Topic: solutions **3.**
buses to airport	

airline food	
late departures	Topic: in-flight problems **2.**
small seats	

Step 4: Launch into the First Draft

After planning, brainstorming, and organizing, you're ready to write your first draft. Here arc some suggestions.

As you write, aim to include everything that's consistent with your plan—the facts and figures, dates and times, recommendations and conclusions.

Drafting is a "right-brain" task. Do it quickly—as quickly as you can write. Ignore the rules of grammar, spelling, punctuation, and capitalization. Get the words down. A useful guideline is: First get it down, then get it right. By saving the editing for later, you can produce better work in less total time.

You will learn Step 5: Revise & Edit in the next lesson.

Practice

Follow the steps in this exercise to plan, brainstorm, organize, and draft an essay of about 250 words. You may pick any topic. To focus on the new writing process, it is probably better to choose some familiar topic, rather than an actual assignment from one of your other courses. But, that would be OK, too. There is a list of suggested topics below.

Use this space below for your plan, your Keywords, and your Key Sentences or Clusters. Then do your draft on separate sheets of paper.

1. Plan. Define your:

Audience_____

Purpose_____

Topic _____

Specific Requirements _____

2. Brainstorm. Jot down your Keywords.

_____

_____

_____

_____

_____

3. Organize. Write Key Sentences and number them in a logical order. Or Cluster the Keywords and number the Clusters in order.

_____

_____

_____

_____

_____

_____

_____

_____

4. On separate sheets of paper or your computer or laptop, write your draft. It should be about 250 words. Use double or triple spacing so you'll have lots of room for later editing.

Mastery Criteria

To check your mastery of the techniques in this lesson, your professor will ask to see your

- Plan
- Keywords
- Key Sentences or Clusters, numbered in a logical sequence.
- Draft

Your professor will not correct your draft for grammar, punctuation, or spelling. Neither should you. That comes in the next lesson on revising and editing.

Lesson 9

Revise & Edit

Your Own Writing

Almost no one produces finished copy on the first try. Even professional writers write a rough draft and then revise and edit it. When editing his famous novel, *A Farewell to Arms*, Hemingway rewrote the ending 39 times. So, revising and editing is a standard part of producing good writing.

However, in middle and high school, it is common for the students to write and for the teacher to correct. As a result, you may have had little instruction or practice in editing. That's what you will learn in this lesson.

Using Proof Marks for Faster Editing

4 Editing Rules

Using the Writing Process During Tests

How About Term Papers?

Using Proof Marks

for Faster Editing

There are some standard symbols professionals use to revise and edit. These are called proof marks. Using proof marks will help you do a better job, faster.

Some of the most common and useful proof marks are described in the chart at right. These are fairly standard symbols, and most professors and writers will understand them. If you don't understand a professor's proof marks on your papers, ask for clarification.

Study the chart for a few minutes to see what the marks mean. Then begin to use the proof marks in the editing exercises that follow. After

PROOF MARK	MEANING	EXAMPLE
⊙	Insert period.	He wrote well⊙
∧	Insert at this point.	He wote well.
≡	Capitalize this letter.	he wrote well.
/	Make this letter lower case.	He Wrote well.
#	Insert a space.	Hewrote well.
V	Insert an apostrophe or quotation marks.	I wrote well, he said. I He was fortunate.
#▷	Insert new copy here.	He wrote well.
ℓ	Delete.	He wrfote well.
⊓⊔	Transpose.	He well wrote
C	Close up.	He wr te well.
¶	Start new paragraph.	¶ He wrote well.
↘	Move to some other place.	He wrote well and she wrote well.

using the symbols from the chart a few times, you will probably have them memorized.

Even if you write using a computer, most writers and editors do their editing on a printout, rather than on the screen. We suggest that you do this, too, using these proof marks.

Revise, then Edit

In this book, the words revise and edit are separate tasks in the Revise and Edit step of the writing process. Revising means checking the content and sequence of your first draft. At this point, you make additions and deletions of sentences and paragraphs. You may also decide to rearrange the paragraphs. When revising, you ignore spelling, punctuation, and grammar.

When you are satisfied with your revisions, then you edit, sentence by sentence. We will get to the details of editing soon.

What to Do When You Revise

To revise a draft, you read it while paying attention to:

- Sequence
- Completeness
- Accuracy
- Logic

Practice

Do this practice with your draft paper from Lesson 8. If your draft is on your word processor, print it out and work on the paper copy.

- Read the paper and look for ways to improve it by such things as:
  - Add sentences and paragraphs to present material omitted in the draft.
  - Delete sentences and paragraphs that are unnecessary or repetitious.
  - Rearrange sentences or paragraphs to make the order more logical or interesting.
- Use proof marks to mark any additions, deletions, and rearrangements of sentences and paragraphs on the paper copy.

Feedback

After you have revised your draft, the next step is to edit.

4 Editing Rules

Though some people believe editing is only a matter of opinion, there is a lot of agreement among professional editors. We will focus on four editing rules that most editors agree with and which will enable you to do a great job of editing your own writing.

- Use complete sentences.
- Use the active voice.
- Delete unnecessary words.
- Use a spell-checker, dictionary, thesaurus, and a style guide to improve your word choice, spelling, grammar, punctuation, and capitalization.

These rules are not laws. You can violate them. But if you want top grades, don't break the rules carelessly; only when you consciously decide to.

As you work through this lesson, you will learn to apply these rules one at a time.

Rule 1 Use complete sentences

The first editing strategy is to be sure that every sentence is complete. A complete sentence must have at least one subject, one verb, and express a complete thought. There may be more than one subject, verb, or thought in a sentence.

In some sentences, the subject may be omitted. That is grammatically OK if the omitted word is understood. For example, in commands or requests, we frequently omit the word you:

> Tell me what time it is, please.

Here the subject—you—is understood. The sentence means:

> You tell me what time it is, please.

You can probably already spot incomplete sentences. If so, the following exercises can refresh your memory and warm you up as an editor. If you have questions, ask your professor for help.

Practice

Next to each of the following that is a complete sentence write the letter C; next to incomplete sentences write the letter I.

	a.	The paper bag broke.
	b.	Fire is dangerous.
	c.	Your recent, long letter to Ms. Williams.
	d.	Go to the back of the line.
	e.	He fixed.
	f.	The big red barn at the intersection of this street and the highway.
	g.	In trying to explain all the possibilities to the students, the professor's long-winded explanation.
	h.	Wherever you go in this world.
	i.	Do you know?
	j.	Knowing full well that he wasn't telling the truth.
	k.	Regardless of the circumstances, it is impressive to use good grammar.
	l.	One is enough.
	m.	Once upon a time and far, far away.

Feedback

C	a.	The paper bag broke.
C	b.	Fire is dangerous.
I	c.	Your recent, long letter to Ms. Williams.
C	d.	Go to the back of the line.
I	e.	He fixed.
I	f.	The big red barn at the intersection of this street and the highway.
I	g.	In trying to explain all the possibilities to the students, the professor's long-winded explanation.
I	h.	Wherever you go in this world.
C	i.	Do you know?
I	j.	Knowing full well that he wasn't telling the truth.
C	k.	Regardless of the circumstances, it is impressive to use good grammar.
C	l.	One is enough.
I	m.	Once upon a time and far, far away.

If you have any questions about the complete and incomplete sentences, ask your professor.

Practice

Working with a printed or handwritten copy of your draft, examine it sentence by sentence. Is every sentence complete? If not, edit any incomplete sentence to make it a complete sentence. Use proof marks in your editing.

Rule 2 Use the active voice

There are two "voices" in English grammar: the active voice and the passive voice. In the active voice, the subject is doing the action:

> John hit the ball.

In the passive voice, the action is being done to the subject. For example:

The ball was hit by John.

The passive voice is grammatically correct and has its uses. The active voice is clearer and has more "punch." When you edit, first find any passive sentences. Then decide whether to leave them as is or change them to active sentences.

In the passive voice, the action of the verb is done to the subject of the sentence. To spot the passive voice, you:

- Identify the action.
- Identify the subject of the sentence.
- Decide if the action is done to the subject.

Identifying the Action

Verbs are words that express action. Examples are:

run, runs, ran
feel, feels, felt
decide, decides, decided

The actions expressed by these verbs are:
running
feeling
deciding

Practice

What is the action in each of the following sentences? Use the "—ing" form of the word.

SENTENCE	ACTION
Example: John hit the ball.	hitting
John is painting the house.	
Who built the house?	
He thinks of her every day.	
The concrete was poured on Thursday.	
The car had been driven over 100 miles.	

Feedback

SENTENCE	ACTION
Example: John hit the ball.	hitting
John is painting the house.	painting
Who built the house?	building
He thinks of her every day.	thinking
The concrete was poured on Thursday.	pouring
The car had been driven over 100 miles.	driving

Sentences without Action

Some sentences have no action. For example:

> The ball is red.
> The man was tall.
> You are late.
> I am sick.

You might say that these sentences are neither active nor passive. However, since they are not passive, editors consider them active and in compliance with the rule to use the active voice.

The above sentences use some form of the verb "to be." But, the presence or absence of "to be" in any form does not necessarily make a sentence active and passive. For example, "to be" is a helping verb in these sentences:

> Active Voice Example: He has been running five miles every day.
> Passive Voice Example: The dog has been fed every day.

There are actions in these sentences, namely running and feeding. So, in looking for passive sentences, identify the action. If there is no action, consider the sentence active.

Practice

Write the action indicated in each of the following sentences. If there is no action, write "None."

SENTENCE	ACTION
The house is red.	
He is painting the house red.	
The house had been painted red.	
The report is long.	
The report has been prepared by Charlie.	

Feedback

SENTENCE	ACTION
The house is red.	None
He is painting the house red.	painting
The house had been painted red.	painting
The report is long.	None
The report has been prepared by Charlie.	preparing

You should now be able to identify the action in a sentence. If you can't, talk to your professor.

Identifying the Subject

The subject of a sentence is the person or thing the sentence is about. Take this sentence as an example:

> Fred's house is made of wood.

Three things are mentioned: Fred, house, and wood. This sentence is about the house. House is the subject.

When you give a command, the person you are speaking to is the subject of the command. Whether or not you mention any names, the person you command is the subject.

Examples:

> Richard, bring me the book.
> Bring me the book.
> You throw it away.
> Throw it away.

Subjects often come at the beginning of a sentence, but not in questions. In either case, to determine the subject, ask yourself what the sentence is about.

Here are some more examples:

SENTENCE	SUBJECT
The sign was carried by a striker	sign
John was carrying the sign.	John
John's hair grew quickly.	hair
It does not concern you.	it
Give it to me.	you

Practice

In the blanks provided, write in the subjects in the following sentences:

SENTENCE	SUBJECT
Did you build the house?	
Who bought it?	
Why did you do it?	
When was the house built by Charlie?	
By whom was it bought?	

Feedback

SENTENCE	SUBJECT
Did you build the house?	you
Who bought it?	who
Why did you do it?	you
When was the house built by Charlie?	house
By whom was it bought?	it

If you are having trouble, see your professor.

Deciding If the Action Is Done to the Subject

Now you can spot the subject and action of a sentence. All that remains is to decide whether the action is being done by the subject or to the subject. If the subject is doing the action, the sentence is active. If the action is being done to the subject, the sentence is passive. Here are some examples.

The book was read by many people.

- Subject: book
- Action: reading
- Passive: Yes

This sentence is passive. The "reading" is being done to the book, not by it.

I am reading a book.

- Subject: I
- Action: reading
- Passive: No (Active)

Fred is painting the house.

- Subject: Fred
- Action: painting
- Passive: No

Here the painting is being done by Fred. It is not being done to him.

If the action is done to or on the subject, the sentence is passive. If the subject is doing the action, the sentence is active. If there is no action, the sentence is not active nor passive. But since we are mainly concerned about avoiding the passive voice, these sentences don't have to be edited. For editing purposes, we consider them active.

Practice

In the blanks provided, write the subject, the action (in "-ing" form), and indicate active or passive for each of the sentences.

John was carrying the sign.

    Subject: _____

    Action: _____

    Passive: _____

The sign was carried by a striker.

    Subject: _____

    Action: _____

    Passive: _____

The report was written by Charlie.

    Subject: _____

    Action: _____

    Passive: _____

The report was written in English.

    Subject: _____

    Action: _____

    Passive: _____

Feedback

John was carrying the sign.

- Subject: John
- Action: carrying
- Passive: No

The sign was carried by a striker.

- Subject: sign
- Action: carrying
- Passive: Yes

The report was written by Charlie.

- Subject: report
- Action: writing
- Passive: Yes

The report was written in English.

- Subject: report
- Action: writing
- Passive: Yes

Practice

The report is in English

     Subject:

     Action: _____

     Passive: _____

     _____

It will be excellent.

     Subject:

     Action: _____

     Passive: _____

     _____

Who bought it?

     Subject:

     Action: _____

     Passive: _____

     _____

By whom was it bought?

     Subject:

     Action: _____

     Passive: _____

     _____

Show him the book.

     Subject:

     Action: _____

     Passive: _____

     _____

Feedback

The report was in English.

> Subject: report
> Action: None
> Passive: No

It will be excellent.

> Subject: it
> Action: None
> Passive: No

Who bought it?

> Subject: who
> Action: buying
> Passive: No

By whom was it bought?

> Subject: it
> Action: buying
> Passive: Yes

Show him the book.

> Subject: you
> Action: showing
> Passive: No

You should now be able to identify sentences in the passive voice. If you have questions, consult your professor.

When to Use the Passive Voice

The passive voice is useful for setting the tone of a story in creative writing.

> The heavy door was opened by an unseen hand.

The passive voice is also useful for suppressing sensitive information.

> It was learned today from usually reliable sources that the exam will cover only Chapters 7 and 8 of the text.

Practice

Identify any of the following sentences that are in the passive voice. Rewrite those that are passive in the active voice. Finally, for any sentence that you changed from passive to active, put an asterisk (✱) next to the version, active or passive, you prefer.

a. It was a dark and stormy night.

_____

_____

b. The sound of the drawbridge was heard by the people in the town.

_____

_____

c. The full moon was hidden by the clouds.

_____

_____

d. The coffin had been opened by Count Dracula.

_____

_____

e. At the stroke of midnight, the drawbridge was lowered by an unknown person.

_____

_____

Feedback

a.   It was a dark and stormy night.

Active Voice

b.   The sound of the drawbridge was heard by the people in the town.

Passive Voice. Active Voice Rewrite:

>   The people in the town heard the drawbridge. ✱

c.   The full moon was hidden by the clouds.

Passive Voice. Active Voice Rewrite:

>   The clouds hid the full moon. ✱

d.   The coffin had been opened by Count Dracula.

Passive Voice. Active Voice Rewrite:

>   Count Dracula had opened the coffin. ✱

e.   At the stroke of midnight, the drawbridge was lowered by an unknown person.

Passive Voice. Active Voice Rewrite:

>   At the stroke of midnight, an unknown person lowered the drawbridge. ✱

We prefer active sentences in all these cases. If your preference is different, that's OK. The important thing is recognize passive sentences. Then, you can decide whether to change them to active.

Practice
Examine your draft essay, one sentence at a time. For each sentence, determine whether it is active or passive. If the sentence is passive, rewrite it in the active voice. Then decide which version to use.

Feedback
If you have any doubts about identifying and changing passive sentences to active ones, see your professor.

Rule 3 Delete unnecessary words

If you do not load your sentences with extra words, your writing will be clearer and will earn you better grades. Some professors prefer long sentences; some suggest you keep your sentences short. But almost all will disapprove of words that don't add to the meaning.

To find and delete unnecessary words, first read a sentence to find out what it says. Then strike out as many words as possible without losing any meaning.

Here is an example. Read this sentence to find out what it means:

> History is usually thought of as a record of what has happened in the past.

Deleting some words, we get: History is a record of the past.

Or: History is what happened.

These rewrites mean the same as the original. They are also shorter and clearer. All these sentences, including the original, are grammatically correct. When deleting words, make the sentences as brief as possible without losing meaning or turning too many sentences into "Tweets," such as:

> Mom. Send money quick.

Practice

Use proof marks to edit this passage by deleting unnecessary words. Work on one sentence at a time.

The past history of the United States is a record of one of humanity's most noble and impressive efforts to create a society that fairly and equitably serves every single solitary individual person. Some of the ideas and thoughts used by the founders of the United States were taken from the records and history of ancient Greece in the 5th century B.C. Thus, it is not surprising that the architecture of the revolutionary period was largely based upon Greek buildings, palaces, and temples that date from that same golden age of Greek democracy. The U.S. architecture of the Revolutionary period is aptly and appropriately labeled and called Neo-classic—meaning the new version of the classic Greek styles of that period.

Feedback

There are many possibilities. Compare your edit to ours.

The ~~past~~ history of the United States is ~~a record of~~ one of humanity's most noble and impressive efforts to create a society that fairly ~~and equitably~~ serves every ~~single solitary individual~~ person. Some ~~of the~~ ideas ~~and thoughts~~ used by the founders of the United States were taken from ~~the records and history of ancient~~ Greece in the 5th century B.C. Thus, it is not surprising that the architecture of the revolutionary period was ~~largely~~ based upon Greek buildings, palaces, and temples ~~that date~~ from that ~~same~~ golden age of Greek democracy. ~~The~~ U.S. architecture of the Revolutionary period is aptly ~~and appropriately labeled and~~ called Neo-classic ~~meaning the new version of the classic Greek styles of that period~~.

If you have any questions, see your professor.

Practice
Edit your draft by deleting unnecessary words.

Feedback
It is possible that your draft was free of unnecessary words in the first place. That is unlikely for almost any writer. If you didn't find any unnecessary words, check again.

Rule 4 Use a spell-checker, dictionary, thesaurus, and a style guide to improve your spelling, word choice, and grammar.

Spelling, word choice and grammar are important to most editors, college faculty and business people. So, it pays to do a good job on this final step in editing.

Using a spell checker will catch some spelling errors. But, if you use a wrong word, a spell checker will not catch the error. For example, these pairs of words are often confused:

affect / effect	then / than
their / they're	your / you're

All these words are spelled correctly.

In academic writing, use slang only for dialog. Slang includes words such as:

ain't	awesome
cool	dude
gnarly	ginormous

English grammar is based on usage—that is, the way people use language in daily life. There is not an official rule book or authority on usage. Still, some usage is accepted among educated people, and some is not. Your professors—and later your employers or customers—will expect your writing to conform to accepted usage.

You already know a lot of grammar. You use many rules, sometimes by applying a rule, but often just because it sounds right. Still, many of the grammatical constructions we use in everyday speech are not accepted usage for writing. For that reason, using a reference book to check on grammar, punctuation, and capitalization in your writing is essential in college and business.

You might think professional editors never need a grammar reference. Actually, the opposite is true. These people commonly use grammar and style references as they work, along with a dictionary. The rest of us can profit by doing the same.

You can find both a dictionary and a grammar guide for free on the Internet. For example, try **www.dictionary.com** and **http://stylemanual.ngs.org/.** If you prefer to use a printed dictionary or style guide, buy them and keep them handy when you edit. Two excellent grammar references are available in paperback and cost only about $8: *Write Right,* by Jan Vanolia, published by Ten Speed Press; and *Elements of Style,* by Strunk and White, published by MacMillan.

As you use reference books, remember that they might disagree on certain points.

Practice

These practices are to get you familiar with a grammar and style guide. You are not supposed to memorize the book or even the few rules you look up. The point is to learn how to use the book.

1. Read the Table of Contents. If there is an index, look it over to see how it can help you locate information in the book.

2. Look up "that" and "which" to correct this sentence.

     From among those bottles, please hand me the one (that/which) contains water.

3. Check and correct every single point of grammar, spelling, and punctuation in this sentence.

    It was 3:30 A.M. when a terrible noise awakened me and I shouted whose their.

Feedback

1. No answer required.

2. Look up "that" and "which" to correct this sentence.
    o **From among those bottles, please hand me the one ~~which~~/that contains water**.

3. Use a grammar reference and a dictionary to check every single point of grammar, spelling, and punctuation in the two sentences below. Rewrite the sentences correctly.

    It was 3:30 A.M. when a terrible noise awakened me and I shouted whose their.

    It was 3:30 A.M. when a terrible noise awakened me. I shouted, "Who's there?"

Practice

There are about 18 grammar, spelling, and punctuation errors in the paragraph below. Consider one sentence at a time, correcting any errors you find. Use your grammar reference and dictionary, as needed.

MY VACATION

My Brother and Me went to new york last Fall on a vacation. Before we goed, we red a book on new york so we would know what wed like to sea. Then that guidebook was carried to new york by us. That turned out to be really, really very helpful and I think it helped us enjoy the vacation which we did.

Feedback

MY VACATION

My Brother and Me went to new york last fall on a vacation. Before we ~~goed~~ *went*, we ~~red~~ *read* a book on new york so we would know what wed like to ~~sea.~~ *see.* ~~Then~~ *We took* that guidebook ~~was carried~~ to new york ~~by~~ *with* us. That turned out to be ~~really, really~~ very helpful**;** ~~and I think~~ it helped us enjoy the vacation**,** ~~which we did.~~

Practice

Examine each sentence of your essay for grammar and spelling errors. If you find any errors, correct them. If you are uncertain of any point of grammar, use your grammar reference. If you are uncertain of the spelling or meaning of a word, look it up in a dictionary.

This might seem like a lot of work, but it will probably take no more than 10 minutes for a 250-word essay. If it takes longer, then you are probably improving the quality of your paper substantially.

Feedback

Your professor will review your edited essay later. But, if you need help, ask for it now.

Live Feedback

A great source of useful feedback is to get a few classmates or friends to read your paper and give you feedback. That's your next practice.

Practice

Ask two other people—classmates or friends—to read your draft and give you their comments. Ask them to focus on the big issues: the topic, the organization, the level of detail, and the tone. Have them tell you their comments in person or by phone, so you get all the details. Take notes on what they say.

Based on their comments, make any additional revisions.

Feedback

You have now revised and edited your paper. Did you find the feedback from your reviewers helpful?

Summary of the Writing Process

PLAN
- Audience
- Topic
- Purpose
- Specific requirements

BRAINSTORM
- Jot down Keywords

ORGANIZE
- Jot down Key Sentences or Cluster the Keywords.
- Number Key Sentences or Clusters in a logical order.
  - Time Sequence
  - Location or Position
  - Describe, Analyze, Recommend (or Conclude)
  - Overview, Major Facts, Minor Facts

DRAFT

REVISE AND EDIT
- Use complete sentences.
- Use the active voice.
- Delete unnecessary words.
- Check spellings and meanings of words.
- Check questionable grammar, punctuation, and capitalization.

Using the WRITING PROCESS During Tests

Because of time pressure on an essay exam, you may be tempted to skip the steps of the writing process and dive in without a plan. You may also use all the time for writing, leaving no time to revise and edit. But, that is probably not your best strategy. Instead, use the writing process, with the few modifications described below.

Essay examination questions almost always give you the topic and purpose you are to write about. If you have to choose the topic, jot a couple of alternatives and choose. You have no time to waste.

Brainstorm Keywords for no more than one minute. Then, in another minute jot down a couple of Key Sentences and number them in sequence. The next step may take some courage. Following the ideas in the writing process, write your first draft quickly, without correcting spelling, punctuation and grammar errors. The challenge is for you to trust that writing s first draft and then editing it will be faster and better than trying to draft and edit at the same time.

For example, suppose you have four essay questions on a 60-minute exam, each worth 25 points. So, you could allocate 15 minutes to each question. Of that time, imagine you plan and organize for 2 minutes, draft for 8 minutes and edit for 5 minutes. Since most of us write at about 25 words per minute, you might expect to write a 200-word draft in 8 minutes.

Now, the question is whether the process in the example would be better than spending 2 minutes planning and 13 minutes writing and editing in one pass. A third possibility would be to skip the planning and organizing and to spend the whole 15 minutes writing. The following practice should help you decide.

Practice

Choose an essay question from one of your textbooks or a recent exam. Follow this modified writing process in answering the question in 15 minutes:

- 1 minute: Brainstorm Key Words
- 1 minute: Organize with Key Sentences or Clusters of Key Words
- 8 minutes: Write a first draft
- 5 minutes: Revise and Edit

Try it.

Feedback

What do you think? Did this work better than what you have done in the past?

How About Term Papers?

Term paper assignments require planning, time management, research, note-taking, organizing, problem-solving, and, of course, writing the paper. The 5-Step Writing Process is especially valuable for longer documents. That is because the process eliminates so much re-arranging and re-writing.

Mastery Criteria

To check your mastery of revising and editing and using the writing process for exams and term papers, your professor will ask you to show:

- Your revised and edited paper from Lesson 8.
- Your 15-minute answer to an essay question.

Your professor will be checking for your mastery of the process, rather than correcting or grading your essay.

Lesson 10

Mastering Math and Science Courses

This lesson has worked for students who have been great at math and those who dread it. It is likely to work for you. In this lesson, you will master two powerful and useful math skills. These skills will help you in any future math and science courses you may take. But even more importantly, you will practice using the Power Learners approach in learning math and science. Mastering this lesson may improve your mindset about your ability to excel in math and science.

What has been your experience with math?

Math is Methods for Solving Problems

Pre-requisites are Essential

Converting Units

Problem-solving

What has been your experience with math?

Have you been a star, done OK but not great, or have you had great difficulty and pain? Before beginning this lesson, take a few minutes to think about your experiences and how they may help or hinder your learning math.

Practice

Describe your past experiences with math. What happened? How did you feel?

_____

_____

_____

_____

What do you think about your ability to learn math?

_____

_____

_____

How do you feel about working on this lesson? Are you willing to begin?

_____

_____

_____

Feedback

Whether you've been a whiz or want to avoid math at all costs, this lesson is likely to make a big change in your ability to learn and like math and science in school and life.

Why Learn Math

Before digging into the specifics of this lesson, a few overview comments about math may be helpful.

First, to operate in life, there are some things we need to know by remembering. These are things like our birthdate and phone number. Then there are the things we need to figure out by applying logic to a set of facts. For example, if you buy shoes for $87.59 and you give the clerk a $100 bill, how much change should you get? Maybe you can do this in your head. Maybe you would use a calculator. Either way, the point is that you don't remember the amount of change. You figure it out.

For some kinds of problems, we use facts and logic, but no math. An example would be figuring out what to buy your mom for her birthday. In other fields, scientists, engineers, and others use various mathematical methods to apply facts and logic to solve problems. Over the centuries, mathematicians have developed thousands of problem-solving methods. There are so many methods in math that no one knows them all.

Of course, not everyone uses math in their careers and life. Still, educators include math in the required curriculum for everyone. Here are some possible reasons.

- Basic math and problem-solving are essential in the modern world.

- Math courses are a good way to learn logical thinking and problem-solving. You may forget the math, but the thinking and problem-solving are useful in general.

- It takes years to learn the math needed to begin studying some technical subjects. So, schools and colleges have courses in the math needed for those fields.

Practice

1. Consider this question:

   In what year did Columbus make his most famous expedition?

Do you answer this question by remembering or by problem-solving?

   Remembering   Problem-solving

2. Suppose that you work in a bicycle shop. A customer comes in and buys one mountain bike and one road bike. The manager says to you, "Give the customer a discount of 8.5%." How does the manager expect you to solve the problem?

   a. By remembering how much a mountain bike and road bike cost after a discount of 8.5%.

   b. By figuring out the amount in your head.

   c. By figuring out the amount with a calculator or computer.

3. Math includes:

   a. Mental techniques for solving problems in your head.

   b. Using symbols and methods to solve problems that are too difficult to do in your head.

   c. A large number of methods for solving various types of problems.

   d. All of the above.

4. After completing the math and science requirements for a bachelor's degree, is it likely you will have to learn additional math in your career?

Feedback

1. Consider this question:

> In what year did Columbus make his most famous expedition?

Do you answer this question by remembering or by problem-solving?

Remembering   Problem-solving

A historian might figure out the year by consulting old records. But most of us know this fact simply by remembering it.

2. Suppose that you work in a bicycle shop. A customer comes in and buys one mountain bike and one road bike. The manager says to you, "Give the customer a discount of 8.5%." How does the manager expect you to solve the problem?

    a. By remembering how much a mountain bike and road bike cost after a discount of 8.5%.

    b. By figuring out the amount in your head.

    c. By figuring out the amount with a calculator or computer.

Some stores have cash registers connected to a computer system that reads the UPC on the price tag and computes any discounts automatically. In other stores, the salespeople use handheld calculators.

3. Math includes:

    a. Mental techniques for solving problems in your head.

    b. Using symbols and methods to solve problems that are too difficult to do in your head.

    c. A large number of methods for solving various types of problems.

    d. All of the above.

4. After completing the math and science requirements for a bachelor's degree, is it likely you will have to learn additional math in your career?

Yes. With the increased importance of technology in all fields, we think you are likely to have to learn additional math methods throughout your career.

Why are there Weird Problems in Math Courses

In math courses like algebra, you get problems such as this:

Mary is three times as old as Jane.

The sum of their ages is 48.

How old are they?

(Don't solve this problem. It's an example).

Problems like this may seem weird. Other than possibly at a job interview for a high-tech company, when would you ever bump into someone who presented information this way? So, why do math books have problems like this?

Here's one answer: In math, you learn techniques that can be used to solve real-world problems. But those real problems are in fields like electronics or economics which you may study in the future. Since you can't yet understand those real problems, they would make learning the math more difficult. To avoid that, math professors use problems you can understand, even if those problems are unrealistic.

Practice

Here's a typical word-problem from algebra.

The sum of three consecutive, odd integers is 255. What are those integers?

(Don't solve this problem. It's just an example.)

Which of these do you consider an important reason for learning to solve this type of problem?

a.   Integer problems are useful in many professions.

b.   Every well-educated person needs to know how to solve integer problems.

e.   The logic and methods for solving integer problems are useful in various technical and non-technical fields.

Feedback

Here's a typical word-problem from algebra.

The sum of three consecutive odd integers is 255. What are those integers?

(Don't solve this problem. It's just an example.)

Which of these do you consider an important reason for learning to solve this type of problem?

a.   Integer problems are useful in many professions.

b.   Every well-educated person needs to know how to solve integer problems.

c.   The logic and methods for solving integer problems are needed in various technical and non-technical fields.

Learning How to Master Math and Science Courses

The remainder of this lesson consists of three sections. As a preview, here are descriptions and the intended purposes of the three sections.

Section 10A – Fractions

We start with fractions for two reasons.

- You will experience that pre-requisites are critical. The skills with fractions in Section 10A are essential for learning to convert units in Section 10B. These skills are also essential for Algebra and subsequent math courses.
- You will find that learning or reviewing a pre-requisite may only take you minutes rather than days.

Section 10B – Converting Units

In Section 10B you will learn a great method for converting units. The purposes for doing this are:

- The method you will learn is extremely useful in math and science courses

- This is the method that most scientists and engineers use in their work. Still, almost no one learns this method in high school or college. It will almost certainly be new to you.

- Mastering Unit Conversions is a real accomplishment. We hope it will give you a feeling of success and a positive mindset about your ability to learn math.

Section 10C – Problem-solving

When confronted with a problem to solve on a test or in life, students often feel stuck. They don't know how to proceed. This section contains two keys to getting over this barrier in problem-solving. These keys are useful in math and also in any problem-solving, whether it involves math or not. Again, the purpose of this section is for you to improve at problem-solving and to experience success in learning math.

Section 10A – Fractions

You are going to learn to multiply, divide and simplify fractions, starting from scratch. So, though you may have to think hard, you won't be blocked if you don't remember this math that you probably had in middle school. Regardless of your history with math, please don't give up. If you need help, ask your professor. Then, continue practicing until you master this pre-requisite for what comes later.

A fraction is a number written as, for example, $\frac{3}{5}$

As you know, this fraction means 3 divided by 5. Doing the math in your head, with a calculator or by long division with a pencil and paper, you can calculate the value of 3 divided by 5:

$$\frac{3}{5} = 0.6$$

Multiply Fractions

Here is the general rule for multiplying fractions:

$$\frac{a}{b} \times \frac{c}{d} = \frac{ac}{bd}$$

In this formula, a, b, c, and d stand for any numbers. They can be whole numbers or decimals or fractions. Each number can also be positive or negative.

Note: Mathematical notation doesn't define the value of a number divided by 0. So, in the multiplication formula, neither b nor d can be zero.

Example:

$$\frac{1}{2} \times \frac{3}{5} = \frac{1 \times 3}{2 \times 5} = \frac{3}{10}$$

Practice

Using a pen or pencil, write your answers to these two problems:

$$\frac{3}{7} \times \frac{4}{5} =$$

$$\frac{a}{e} \times \frac{p}{t} =$$

Feedback

$$\frac{3}{7} \times \frac{4}{5} = \frac{12}{35}$$

$$\frac{a}{e} \times \frac{p}{t} = \frac{ap}{et}$$

Talking About Math

When you are learning math, it helps to talk to yourself as you do the various steps of a problem. For example, when you are learning to add, you may have said to yourself, "Two plus three are five." As another example, in Algebra, you may have said something like this, "Divide both sides of the equation by 10." Well, this "self-talk" is useful in math. Even experienced mathematicians do it to "talk themselves through" solving problems.

To prepare to "talk yourself through" using fractions, it will help to understand and use the right words.

Let's start with this. A fraction is one quantity divided by another. Mathematicians call the top quantity the "numerator" and the bottom quantity the "denominator."

$$\frac{3}{5} \quad \frac{\text{NUMERATOR}}{\text{DENOMINATOR}}$$

The number 3 is the numerator. The number 5 is the denominator. To help you remember these names, think: the nUmerator is UP and the Denominator is DOWN.

$$\frac{\overset{\text{P}}{\text{NUMERATOR}}}{\underset{\begin{smallmatrix}\text{O}\\\text{W}\\\text{N}\end{smallmatrix}}{\text{DENOMINATOR}}}$$

One more thing. The line in a fraction means "divided by." So, in words, a fraction is the "numerator divided by the denominator."

Practice

Say the fraction $\frac{3}{7}$ in words.

Say the fraction $\frac{a}{b}$ in words.

Feedback

Say the fraction $\dfrac{3}{7}$ in words. **"Three divided by seven."**

If you do a lot of math sometime in the future, you can safely call divided-by by its nickname "over," without getting confused. For now, we suggest you say, "Three divided by seven," rather than "Three over seven."

Say the fraction $\dfrac{a}{b}$ in words. **"a divided by b."**

Simplifying Fractions

You can calculate the value of a fraction using a calculator or long division. For example, $\dfrac{1}{2} = 0.5$. Also, you can calculate $\dfrac{2}{4} = 0.5$. From this, you can see that ½ and 2/4 are equal in value. Mathematicians provide us with this general rule:

> Multiplying the numerator and denominator of a fraction by the same number does not change the value of the fraction.

$$\frac{a}{e} = \frac{ab}{eb}$$

Here's an example.

$$\frac{3}{7} = 0.4285$$

Multiplying numerator and denominator by 2:

$$\frac{3}{7} = \frac{3 \times 2}{7 \times 2} = \frac{6}{14} = 0.4285$$

This also works in reverse. Dividing the numerator and denominator of a fraction by the same number does not change the value of the fraction.

$$\frac{ab}{eb} = \frac{a}{e}$$

Here's an example of dividing the numerator and denominator by the same number:

$$\frac{6}{14} = \frac{\frac{6}{2}}{\frac{14}{2}} = \frac{3}{7} = 0.4285$$

Practice

Simplify these fractions. As you do each problem, talk yourself through each step.

$$\frac{8}{24}$$

$$\frac{ab}{ac}$$

Feedback

"Divide the numerator and the denominator by 8."

$$\frac{8}{24} = \frac{1}{3}$$

"Divide the numerator and the denominator by a."

$$\frac{ab}{ac} = \frac{b}{c}$$

Divide Fractions

In this section, you are going to review or learn to divide fractions. Even though you may already know a method for dividing fractions, please learn this method. Later in this lesson, you will see that this method is very useful in applying math to science courses and the real world.

Let's begin by writing one fraction divided by another fraction like this:

$$\frac{\frac{1}{2}}{\frac{3}{5}}$$

Here we have the fraction ½ divided by the fraction 3/5. There's a neat and useful way to figure out what this means. Suppose we multiply numerator and denominator by 5/3.

$$\frac{\frac{1}{2}}{\frac{3}{5}} = \frac{\frac{1}{2} \times \frac{5}{3}}{\frac{3}{5} \times \frac{5}{3}} = \frac{\frac{5}{6}}{\frac{15}{15}}$$

Now, we first notice that 15/15 = 1.

$$\frac{\frac{5}{6}}{\frac{15}{15}} = \frac{\frac{5}{6}}{1}$$

But any number divided by 1 is the number itself.

$$\frac{\frac{5}{6}}{1} = \frac{5}{6}$$

This wasn't an accident. We got here by multiplying the numerator and denominator of the original "double" fraction by 5/3.

$$\frac{\frac{1}{2}}{\frac{3}{5}} = \frac{\frac{1}{2} \times \frac{5}{3}}{\frac{3}{5} \times \frac{5}{3}}$$

We chose to multiply by 5/3 because 3/5 x 5/3 =15/15 = 1. This works in general for any fraction:

$$\frac{c}{d} \times \frac{d}{c} = \frac{cd}{dc} = \frac{cd}{cd} = 1$$

In words, if you multiply a fraction by the flip of that fraction, you always get 1. In case you are interested, mathematicians call the flip of a fraction its "reciprocal."

So, to simplify a compound fraction, the method is to multiply the numerator and denominator by the reciprocal of the denominator:

$$\frac{\frac{a}{b}}{\frac{c}{d}} = \frac{\frac{a}{b} \times \frac{d}{c}}{\frac{c}{d} \times \frac{d}{c}} = \frac{\frac{ad}{bc}}{\frac{cd}{dc}} = \frac{\frac{ad}{bc}}{1} = \frac{ad}{bc}$$

Here is a complete example:

$$\frac{\frac{1}{2}}{\frac{3}{5}} = \frac{\frac{1}{2} \times \frac{5}{3}}{\frac{3}{5} \times \frac{5}{3}} = \frac{\frac{5}{6}}{\frac{15}{15}} = \frac{\frac{5}{6}}{1} = \frac{5}{6}$$

Practice

Simplify the fraction 2/5 divided by 3/7.

$$\frac{\frac{2}{5}}{\frac{3}{7}}$$

Feedback

Say to yourself, "multiply numerator and denominator by the reciprocal of the denominator. Do the multiplications. Notice that 21/21 = 1. Finally, any number divided by 1 is just the number itself.

$$\frac{\frac{2}{5}}{\frac{3}{7}} = \frac{\frac{2}{5} \times \frac{7}{3}}{\frac{3}{7} \times \frac{7}{3}} = \frac{\frac{14}{15}}{\frac{21}{21}} = \frac{\frac{14}{15}}{1} = \frac{14}{15}$$

Practice

To be sure you have mastered these skills with fractions, do these two additional practice exercises.

1. Simplify the fraction 4/31 divided by 1/5.

$$\frac{\dfrac{4}{31}}{\dfrac{1}{5}}$$

2. Simplify the fraction f/g divided by p/r, where f, g, p, and r stand for any quantities.

$$\frac{\dfrac{f}{g}}{\dfrac{p}{r}}$$

Feedback

1. Simplify the fraction 4/31 divided by 1/5.

$$\frac{\frac{4}{31}}{\frac{1}{5}}$$

Say to yourself, "multiply numerator and denominator by the reciprocal of the denominator. Do the multiplications. Notice that 21/21 = 1. Finally, any number divided by 1 is just the number itself."

$$\frac{\frac{4}{31}}{\frac{1}{5}} = \frac{\frac{4}{31} \times \frac{5}{1}}{\frac{1}{5} \times \frac{5}{1}} = \frac{\frac{20}{31}}{\frac{5}{5}} = \frac{\frac{20}{31}}{1} = \frac{20}{31}$$

1. Simplify the fraction f/g divided by p/r, where f, g, p, and r stand for any quantities.

$$\frac{\frac{f}{g}}{\frac{p}{r}}$$

$$\frac{\frac{f}{g}}{\frac{p}{r}} = \frac{\frac{f}{g} \times \frac{r}{p}}{\frac{p}{r} \times \frac{r}{p}} = \frac{\frac{fr}{gp}}{\frac{pr}{pr}} = \frac{\frac{fr}{gp}}{1} = \frac{fr}{gp}$$

If you were able to do these practices problems correctly, you have mastered the skills with fractions that you need for the remaining two sections of this lesson. If not, <u>DO NOT PROCEED</u>. See you professor for assistance in gaining these pre-requisites for what follows.

Section 10B – Converting Units

In this section, you will learn to convert units. This means, for example, converting feet to meters or pounds to ounces. There are several good reasons to learn this.

- It is useful in using arithmetic for everyday problems like computing interest on a loan or following a cooking recipe.
- It will help you enormously in learning math or science in the future.

Most likely, the method you will learn now was not taught in your previous math or science courses and will not be taught in courses you may take in the future. That this method is rarely taught is like the fact that editing, which you learned in Lesson 9, is rarely taught in high school. It is not that editing isn't useful. Millions of writers and editors do it every day. But most of them learned outside of their regular courses. The method you will learn for converting units is the method millions of engineers, physicists, chemists, and other technical people use every day. Using units when applying formulas in science courses is a real aid in understanding the science and avoiding mistakes. Several thousand of our students have found this lesson helpful in making a new start in learning and using math in school and life.

Using Units

You are probably familiar with quantities such as these:

> 2 pounds (of hamburger)
>
> $4.38 (4.38 dollars)
>
> 15 miles per hour

Each of these quantities has two elements: a numerical value and units. The value is a number, and the units are expressed in words. The value tells us how many things there are. The units tell us what kind of things they are.

Practice

1. In the quantity 55 miles per hour, the value is _____ and the units are _____.   .

2. True or false? All times, speeds, distances, areas, temperatures, ages, and prices have units.

           True   False

3. In each of the following cases, write the units. In most cases, there is more than one possible answer. Any correct units will be OK.

CATEGORY	UNITS
Time	hours (or minutes or seconds)
Temperature	
Speed	
Distance	
Age	
Prices	
Area	

Feedback

1. In the quantity 55 miles per hour, the value is _____**55**_____ and the units are
<u>miles per hour</u>   .   .

2. True or false? All times, speeds, distances, areas, temperatures, ages, and prices have units.

True   False

3. In each of the following cases, write the units. In most cases, more than one answer is possible. Any correct units will be OK.

CATEGORY	UNITS
Time	hours (or minutes or seconds)
Temperature	degrees Fahrenheit (or Celsius)
Speed	miles per hour (or kilometers per hour)
Distance	miles (or feet or inches, etc.)
Age	years
Prices	dollars per pound (or cents per apple, etc.)
Area	square feet, etc.

Calculating Units When You Solve Problems

In real-world situations, quantities have both values and units. So, to solve a problem, you calculate both the value and units of the answer. The basic calculations with numbers are adding, subtracting, multiplying, and dividing. So, you need to learn to calculate units for addition, subtraction, multiplication, or division.

Here are the rules to use:

1. Adding: You can only add things with the same units. For example, 3 dollars plus 5 dollars equal 8 dollars. 3 dollars plus 5 cats are not equal to 8 dollar-cats. The best we can say in that case is 3 dollars plus 5 cats. It is meaningless to add the values of quantities with different units. That is why you can only add "like" things.

2. Subtracting: This works the same as adding: You can only subtract quantities with the same units.

3. Multiplying: Multiply the values and the units.
    Example: What is the area of a room that is 12 feet by 30 feet?

    12 feet x 30 feet = 360 feet x feet

    = 360 square feet

4. Dividing: Divide the values and the units.

    Example: If a bicyclist travels 48 miles in 6 hours, what is his average speed?

$$48 \text{ miles} \div 6 \text{ hours} = \frac{48 \text{miles}}{6 \text{ hours}} = \frac{8 \text{ miles}}{\text{hour}}$$
$$= 8 \text{ miles per hour}$$

Practice

A room is 20 feet long by 10 feet wide. What is its area? Calculate both the value and the units of the answer.

Feedback

A room is 20 feet long by 10 feet wide. What is its area? Calculate both the value and the units of the answer.

Area = 20 feet x 10 feet

= 200 feet x feet

= 200 square feet

Fractional Units

Sometimes the units of physical quantities are fractions. For example, the speed of a car might be 55 miles per hour. Here are some different ways of writing that speed:

55 miles per hour

55 mph   [abbreviation]

55 miles/hour [division symbol]

$55 \dfrac{\text{miles}}{\text{hour}}$ [fraction]

The units of speed are miles divided by hours. All the different ways of writing miles per hour are correct. In other words, miles per hour means the same as miles divided by hours, and this can be written as a fraction:

$$\dfrac{\text{miles}}{\text{hour}}$$

For problem-solving, it is usually easiest to write the units as a fraction.

In working with units, you don't have to pay attention to spelling or grammar. We usually say one foot or two feet. We also say, "Give me a two-foot length of rope." So, in all calculations with units, you can assume that the singular (foot) and plural (feet) forms are equivalent and both are OK.

You can also use abbreviations. For example, the price of oranges can be written as:

$$\$3.50 \text{ per dozen} = 3.50 \dfrac{\text{dollars}}{\text{dozen}} = 3.50 \dfrac{\$}{\text{doz}}$$

Practice

A car is traveling at 40 miles per hour. How far will it go in 3 hours?

Feedback

$$40 \, \frac{\text{miles}}{\text{hour}} \times 3 \text{ hours} = 120 \, \frac{\text{miles x hours}}{\text{hours}} = 120 \text{ miles}$$

Multiply the values and the units. In calculating hours x miles/hour, divide the numerator and denominator by hours, to get the result in miles.

Conversion factors

In real-world problems, it is often necessary to convert a quantity from one kind of units to another. Say that we are going to add:

18 inches plus 3 feet

Here we must first convert one quantity to the same units as the other:

1.5 feet + 3 feet = 4.5 feet

or

18 inches + 36 inches = 54 inches

You are now going to learn a systematic way to convert the units of quantities. First notice that unit conversions are based on simple equations such as:

12 inches = 1 foot

4 quarts = 1 gallon

60 seconds = 1 minute

From these simple equations, we notice that the following conversion factors have the value of 1:

$$\frac{12 \text{ inches}}{1 \text{ foot}} = 1 \qquad \frac{4 \text{ quarts}}{1 \text{ gallon}} = 1 \qquad \frac{60 \text{ seconds}}{1 \text{ minute}} = 1$$

These conversion factors have numerators and denominators that are the same real size. The values are different, and the units are different. Still, in each case, the length or volume or time in the numerator equals the quantity in the denominator. That's why these fractional conversion factors have a value of 1.

Multiplying or dividing a quantity by 1 leaves it unchanged. This means we can multiply or divide any quantity by a conversion factor without changing its real value.

Example: Convert 96 inches to feet.

$$96 \text{ inches} \times \frac{1 \text{ foot}}{12 \text{ inches}} = \frac{96 \text{ inches feet}}{12 \text{ inches}}$$

You get the result by dividing the numerator and denominator by inches:

$$96 \text{ inches} \times \frac{1 \text{ foot}}{12 \text{ inches}} = \frac{96 \text{ inches feet}}{12 \text{ inches}} = \frac{96}{12} \text{ feet} = 8 \text{ feet}$$

When you use conversion factors, write the problem exactly as shown here. This way of writing the problem is an important part of the method.

Example: Convert 17 feet to inches.

$$17 \text{ feet} \times \frac{12 \text{ inches}}{1 \text{ foot}} = 204 \text{ inches}$$

For any given pair of units, there are two conversion factors. They are the same except one is flipped over:

$$\text{Example: } \frac{1 \text{ yard}}{3 \text{ feet}} \text{ or } \frac{3 \text{ feet}}{1 \text{ yard}}$$

Since the numerator and denominator are the same in each fraction, each of these conversion factors has a value of 1.

Now here's where you can start thinking like a mathematician. Since conversion factors always come in pairs, you must decide which one to use. One way to do that is to try both and see which one works. But, after you have a little experience, you will usually be able to choose the one that will work first. If it works, you're all set. If it doesn't, try the other.

Again, let's use converting feet to yards as an example. Though you can probably do this example in your head, please hold on. Consider the two possible conversion factors you might use: 1 yard/3 feet and 3 feet/1 yard.

Example: Convert 36 feet to yards.

The conversion factors between feet and yards are:

$$\frac{1 \text{ yard}}{3 \text{ feet}} \text{ and } \frac{3 \text{ feet}}{1 \text{ yard}}$$

Try: $36 \text{ feet} \times \frac{1 \text{ yard}}{3 \text{ feet}} = 36 \text{ yards}$

And try: $36 \text{ feet} \times \frac{3 \text{ feet}}{1 \text{ yard}} = \frac{108 \text{ square-feet}}{\text{yards}}$

Notice that the first conversion factor worked. The units of feet canceled out, and the answer has the desired units of yards. In the second case, the units do not simplify. The calculation is accurate, but not useful. This is not a mistake. It is simply an attempt that didn't work. That's kind of like a detective investigating a suspect in a crime. If the detective can prove that the suspect is innocent, that's good detective work, not a mistake. The fact that the detective must do more work to find the guilty person is part of the job.

Practice

In the following problems, first write a pair of conversion factors, such as:

$$\frac{1 \text{ yard}}{3 \text{ feet}} \quad \text{and} \quad \frac{3 \text{ feet}}{1 \text{ yard}}$$

Then try both conversion factors to see which one works to get the answer requested.

1. Convert 15.6 yards to feet. (There are 3 feet in one yard.)

2. Convert 10,000 grams to pounds. (There are 454 grams in one pound.)

Feedback

1. Convert 15.6 yards to feet

The conversion factors are:

$$\frac{1 \text{ yard}}{3 \text{ feet}} \text{ and } \frac{3 \text{ feet}}{1 \text{ yard}}$$

$$15.6 \text{ yards} \times \frac{1 \text{ yard}}{3 \text{ feet}} = 5.2 \frac{\text{square yards}}{\text{feet}}$$

$$15.6 \text{ yards} \times \frac{3 \text{ feet}}{1 \text{ yard}} = 46.8 \text{ feet}$$

2. Convert 10,000 grams to pounds

The conversion factors are:

$$\frac{454 \text{ grams}}{1 \text{ pound}} \text{ and } \frac{1 \text{ pound}}{454 \text{ grams}}$$

$$10,000 \text{ grams} \times \frac{454 \text{ grams}}{1 \text{ pound}} = 4,540,000 \frac{\text{grams squared}}{\text{pounds}}$$

$$10,000 \text{ grams} \times \frac{1 \text{ pound}}{454 \text{ grams}} = 22.02 \text{ pounds}$$

Section 10C Problem-solving

As already mentioned, math is a collection of methods for solving problems by applying logic to facts, in your head, on paper or with a calculator or computer. Further, there are more methods than anyone can learn. In math and science courses, you learn some methods for solving some problems. So, in applying apply math or logic to a problem in school or life, you face the issue of which method to use. This section provides an opportunity for you to improve at that skill.

Trial and Error

In *Section 10B, Converting Units*, you used a trial-and-error approach to decide which of two related conversion factors to use. You simply tried both conversion factors and chose the one that gave you a useful answer. Sometimes in problem-solving, trial-and-error is the best that anyone can do.

However, with experience, we can often avoid the inefficiency of trial-and-error and choose a workable method on the first try. This is making an educated guess. When you make an educated guess, keep in mind that you are still in the realm of trial-and-error. If your first guess turns out not to work, try a second method, or even a third.

For the trial-and-error approach to work, it is essential that you check your work. Like editing your writing, checking your math work is part of mastering all methods in math. Your professors may or may not emphasize this, but they all do it and recommend that their students do it.

Educated Guessing

Educated guessing implies learning through practice to look for clues that will improve the accuracy of your guesses.

For example, suppose you are taking a science course, and you need to compare the watts of power from a motor to the horsepower of a gasoline engine. Let's ignore the science and focus on converting the units.

Say, an electric car has a 35,000-Watt motor. For comparison to gasoline engines, convert that to Horsepower. The conversion factors are

$$\frac{745 \text{ Watts}}{1 \text{ HP}} \quad \text{and} \quad \frac{1 \text{ HP}}{745 \text{ Watts}}$$

In Section 10B, you just used trial-and-error, trying both conversion factors. Now, instead, look at the two options and see if you can tell in advance which is likely to get you the answer you want.

Practice

To convert the power of the 35,000-Watt motor to Horsepower, which conversion factor would you try first?

$$\frac{745 \text{ Watts}}{1 \text{ HP}} \quad \text{or} \quad \frac{1 \text{ HP}}{745 \text{ Watts}}$$

Feedback

To convert the power of the 35,000-Watt motor to Horsepower, which conversion factor would you try first?

Answer: $\dfrac{1\text{ HP}}{745\text{ Watts}}$

Were you able to choose the right one in your head? If not, there is no shame in that. Try your first choice and see whether it works.

$$35,000\text{ Watts} \times \frac{1\text{ HP}}{745\text{ Watts}}$$

$$35,000\text{ Watts} \times \frac{745\text{ Watts}}{1\text{ HP}}$$

The first calculation will give you an answer in Horsepower, which is what we want. The second calculation is mathematically valid but not useful.

Practice

Here's more practice. In each case make an educated guess and write the conversion factor you would try first.

Convert 265 inches to yards. (There are 36 inches per yard.)

Convert 40 liters to gallons. (There are 3.8 liters per gallon.)

Convert 50 months to years.

Feedback

Convert 265 inches to yards. $\dfrac{1 \text{ yard}}{36 \text{ inches}}$

$$256 \text{ inches x } \dfrac{1 \text{ yard}}{36 \text{ inches}} = 7.11 \text{ yards}$$

Convert 40 liters to gallons. $\dfrac{1 \text{ gallon}}{3.8 \text{ liters}}$

$$40 \text{ liters X } \dfrac{1 \text{ gallon}}{3.8 \text{ liters}} = 10.5 \text{ gallons}$$

Convert 50 months to years. $\dfrac{1 \text{ year}}{12 \text{ months}}$

$$50 \text{ months X } \dfrac{1 \text{ year}}{12 \text{ months}} = 4.2 \text{ years}$$

Using Several Conversion Factors

Sometimes solving a problem calls for converting units several times.

For example, suppose you want to convert 8000 miles to inches. You probably know the conversion factors for feet to inches:

$$\frac{1 \text{ foot}}{12 \text{ inches}} \quad \text{and} \quad \frac{12 \text{ inches}}{1 \text{ foot}}$$

and you may remember the conversion factors from feet to miles:

$$\frac{1 \text{ mile}}{5280 \text{ feet}} \quad \text{and} \quad \frac{5280 \text{ feet}}{1 \text{ mile}}$$

Using one conversion factor to go from miles to feet, and a second to go from feet to inches, you could calculate:

$$8000 \text{ miles X} \frac{5280 \text{ feet}}{1 \text{ mile}} \text{ X} \frac{12 \text{ inches}}{1 \text{ foot}} = 506{,}880{,}000 \text{ inches}$$

Practice

In this practice, take the time you need to write out the solution, using as many conversion factors as you need to get the answer. Make educated guesses and then check your work. Before looking at the feedback on the next page, work on this problem until you are confident you have the right answer.

Suppose that at top-speed a snail crawls 4 inches per minute. How fast is that in miles per hour?

Feedback

$$4 \frac{\text{inches}}{\text{minute}} \times \frac{1 \text{ foot}}{12 \text{ inches}} \times \frac{1 \text{ mile}}{5280 \text{ feet}} \times \frac{60 \text{ minutes}}{\text{hour}} = 0.0038 \text{ mph}$$

The last practice required three conversion factors. Depending upon how educated your guesses of which conversion factors to use, that practice might have taken quite a while.

To assure that you are mastering educated guesses, please take the time to do these additional practices.

More Practice

Make educated guesses and check your work.

    1. Suppose that hamburger costs 4.50 dollars per pound in the U.S. For comparison to prices in Mexico, convert this price to pesos per kilogram. (1 dollars = 18.5 pesos, and 2.2 pounds = 1 kilogram)

    2. You can estimate how far away a storm is by counting the seconds from when you see a flash of lightning to when you hear the thunder. Since light travels so fast, you can ignore the time it takes for the light of the lightning to reach you. But the sound travels at about 720 miles per hour. How far does the sound travel in one second?

    3. A thoroughbred horse can run 6 furlongs in 73 seconds. How fast is that in miles per hour? (1 mile = 8 furlongs)

Feedback

1. Suppose that hamburger costs 4.50 Dollars per Pound in the U.S. For comparison to prices in Mexico, convert this price to Pesos per Kilogram. (1 Dollar = 18.5 Pesos, and 2.2 Pounds = 1 Kilogram)

$$\frac{4.5 \text{ Dollars}}{\text{Pound}} \text{ X } \frac{18.5 \text{ Pesos}}{1 \text{ Dollar}} \text{ X } \frac{2.2 \text{ Pounds}}{1 \text{ Kilogram}} = \frac{183 \text{Pesos}}{\text{Kilogram}}$$

2. You can estimate how far away a storm is by counting the seconds from when you see a flash of lightning to when you hear the thunder. Since light travels so fast, you can ignore the time it takes for the light of the lightning to reach you. But the sound travels at about 720 miles per hour. How far does sound travel in one second?

$$\frac{720 \text{ Miles}}{\text{Hour}} \text{ X } \frac{1 \text{ Hours}}{60 \text{ Minutes}} \text{X} \frac{1 \text{ minutes}}{60 \text{ Seconds}} = \frac{0.2 \text{ Miles}}{\text{Second}}$$

3. A thoroughbred horse can run 6 furlongs in 73 seconds. How fast is that in miles per hour? (1 Mile = 8 Furlongs)

$$\frac{6 \text{ Furlongs}}{73 \text{ Seconds}} \text{ X } \frac{1 \text{ Miles}}{8 \text{ Furlongs}} \text{X} \frac{60 \text{ Seconds}}{1 \text{ Minute}} \text{ X } \frac{60 \text{ Minutes}}{1 \text{ Hour}} = 37 \frac{\text{Miles}}{\text{Hour}}$$

The Educated Problem-Solver

In math courses, you learn methods by doing the problems at the end of each section or chapter in the textbook. The problems at the end of each section can be solved using the methods presented in that section. So far, so good. But then, on tests, you are likely to find problems from different sections and chapters. You now need to figure out which method to use to solve each problem.

As you found in choosing conversion factors, you can practice and improve at making educated guesses. You can also get used to checking your work and, if necessary, trying a different method. You can do the same in general, and especially in your math and science courses.

As you proceed through a math or science course, make flashcards of the problem-solving methods and formulas you learn. Put a typical problem on one side of the flashcard and the method or formula on the other. As you go through the course, quiz yourself with these flashcards. That practice will build your skills in making better guesses on which method to use for which problem.

Practice

Mark whether each item is True or False.

1. You should expect that your first choice of a technique to solve a problem will always be the best technique for that problem.

> True   False

2. By practicing, you can get more skilled at choosing the method that is likely to solve a problem.

> True   False

3. Checking your solution is an essential part of problem-solving.

> True   False

4. To prepare effectively for the final exam in a math course, you should:
    - Practice solving problems with each of the methods covered in the course.
    - Practice deciding which method to try first to solve the various kinds of problems covered in the course.
    - Both a and b.

Feedback

Mark whether each item is True or False.

1. You should expect that your first choice of a technique to solve a problem will always be the best technique for that problem.

    True   **False**

2. By practicing, you can get more skilled at choosing the method that is likely to solve a problem.

    True False

3. Checking your solution is an essential part of problem-solving.

    True False

4. To prepare effectively for the final exam in a math course, you can:
    a. Practice solving problems with each of the methods covered in the course.
    b. Practice deciding which method to try first to solve the various kinds of problems covered in the course.
    c. **Both a and b.**

Mastery Criterion

Which of these guidelines for learning math do you think will be helpful to you in future math and science courses?

*   Filling any gaps in your pre-requisites is essential and can be quick
*   Mastering every lesson in turn
*   Converting Units
*   Practicing making educated guesses of the method to use for a problem

Discuss your answers with your professor.